MAKING IT
BIG IN
DATA
PROCESSING

Books by Robert Half

THE ROBERT HALF WAY TO GET HIRED IN
  TODAY'S JOB MARKET

ROBERT HALF'S SUCCESS GUIDE FOR
  ACCOUNTANTS

ROBERT HALF ON HIRING

MAKING IT BIG IN DATA PROCESSING

Robert Half

MAKING IT BIG IN DATA PROCESSING

CROWN PUBLISHERS, INC.
NEW YORK

Published by Crown Publishers, Inc., 225 Park Avenue South, New York, New York 10003 and represented in Canada by the Canadian MANDA Group

CROWN is a trademark of Crown Publishers, Inc.

Manufactured in the United States of America

Library of Congress Cataloging-in-Publication Data

Half, Robert.
    Making it big in data processing.

    1. Electronic data processing—Vocational guidance.
2. Electronic data processing personnel. I. Title.
QA76.25.H35 1987   004'.023   86–29316

ISBN 0-517-56580-3

Book design by June Marie Bennett

10 9 8 7 6 5 4 3 2 1

First Edition

To my daughters,
Nancy Asch and Peggy Silbert,
who have brought me so much happiness

CONTENTS

In Appreciation

Many thanks to those who have pitched in
to help me with this book: Donald Bain,
Joan Bernstein, A. Bernard Frechtman,
Alvin Galland, Marc Silbert,
Sanford Teller, James W. Thomas,
Jane von Mehren, and James O. Wade.

INTRODUCTION

*How to navigate the dizzying, tumultuous
world of data processing . . . as a career*

That's what this book is all about.

Twenty years ago data processing didn't represent much of a career choice. That is no longer true. If any industry has grown faster than data processing, I'm at a loss to identify it. More important than the industry's growth, however, is what it has created for us as a society, and for everyone in the workplace.

Data processing is wide open now for career advancement. It is a growth industry in every sense, and the future promises bigger and better opportunities for millions of men and women. The problem—and it's the kind of problem that is inherent in every growth industry—is that while there were only one or two major highways to a successful future ten years ago, roads now lead to hundreds, perhaps thousands, of new and unfamiliar destinations. It's confusing. It's perplexing. It's *dizzying.* And it must be understood by anyone hoping to find success and satisfaction in a data-processing career.

This book has been written to help bring about that understanding.

There's no debate that data processing is one of our leading growth industries. The Bureau of Labor Statistics (BLS) estimates that by 1995 data-processing jobs will increase by at least 35 percent, with more than a million and a half jobs to be filled by that year. (My studies place the number of people *currently* working in data processing at about two million, significantly higher than the BLS estimates. The disparities in such figures reflect differences in the definition of what constitutes a data-processing or computer-related job.)

In another study by an independent research firm, an overwhelming number of respondents from some of the nation's largest corporations agreed that opportunities today are better than ever for data processors. In fact, 94 percent of data-processing managers and top management see the opportunities for DPers expanding significantly, and the field includes opportunities for men and women alike. My own studies indicate that while 64 percent of data-processing and top management surveyed see DP as an excellent field for rapid advancement for men, 77 percent feel that data processing provides a fast-track opportunity for *women*.

The salient point is that the numbers and the opportunities are big. The field is big. The future in data processing is waiting for you—it's up to you to do something about it.

But projections of opportunity represent only one chapter in the DP story, the one dealing with those jobs that are literally defined as belonging to data processing—programmers, systems analysts, equipment repairers, operators, and the like. The even bigger story has to do with the way *all industry* will function in the future, at least according to expert projections. No matter what the business or profession—retailing, medicine, construction, transportation, communications, or service—by 1995 computer technology will be at the core. It's almost there already. The career potential for everyone with data-processing knowledge and skills will increase proportionately.

My decision to write this book reflects my involvement with data processing through more than thirty-five years as a professional in the career aspects of specialized occupations. Focusing on specialties stemmed from an awareness that each specialized occupation is unique and demands an individual approach.

This is certainly true with data processing. The field is too complex and mercurial for its career potentials to be tracked by generalists. That's why my company's over 115 company-owned and franchised offices have experts in data-processing recruiting. The men and women working in data processing—or aspiring to careers in it—have a unique set of demands placed upon them that spring from the field's technological base. Because the data processor deals with both cause and effect—the technology *and* its end result—the trip to the top necessarily involves certain detours and roadblocks that people in other professions don't usually encounter.

At the same time, there are time-honored, universal rules for career success that apply to every profession, including data processing. Accounting, an old profession, provides a good example. Years ago technical competence was often enough for success in the accounting field. But as the importance of accounting grew in every phase of business, the accountant's stock rose with it, which meant that an increasing number of high-level corporate positions opened up to people who understood the accounting function. That situation, however, posed a problem for many accountants who had never bothered to look beyond facts and figures, who were unable or unwilling to view their expertise in the broader context of the corporation's overall needs. Those who could view themselves as businesspeople first and accountants second went far, and continue to succeed.

The parallel with data processing is clear. While technical knowledge and skill are vital for entering the DP field and growing within it, loftier DP management jobs demand a well-rounded individual who combines that technical knowledge with a broader perspective on the company, the industry in which it competes, and the world itself.

I chose the title of this book, *Making It Big in Data Processing*, because "making it big" is open to many interpretations. For some, making it big involves a nine-to-five job with a steady paycheck and the ability to leave the job behind at the end of the day. For others, making it big means climbing that proverbial ladder toward positions of greater responsibility, challenge, and financial reward.

Put another way, the difference basically lies in whether you're content with just a *job* in data processing or are planning to use that job as a springboard to a career. If your goal is the latter, this book should prove to be invaluable in helping you plan for that career. If the job alone is most important to you, reading this book will at least give you some insight into promotion possibilities within a more limited scope of data processing. And you never know when you'll change your mind and decide to take a fling at climbing that ladder.

I've drawn upon numerous resources in preparing this book. One, of course, is the Robert Half International network of offices and the data-processing career experts who operate them.

Another is a series of studies I've commissioned over the years. They were conducted for me by Burke Marketing Research, with whom I've worked closely for a long time.

In addition, I'm a member of the Data Processing Management Association and have received excellent input from the editorial staff of its fine magazine, *Data Management,* as well as from numerous members of the organization who graciously and generously gave me their insights into DP success. I'm grateful to them.

This book is about *you,* because it's *you* who must determine how far you go in this field you've chosen— data processing.

MAKING IT BIG IN DATA PROCESSING

1

WHO ARE YOU?

*Understand yourself first before you try to
understand others.*

Because you're involved in some aspect of data processing for a living (or hope to be), there are probably
some personality traits and professional attitudes that
can safely be applied to you, at least according to the
myriad studies of the DPer as a breed. This is not to
suggest that everyone working in data processing is
stereotypical. In fact, the DP field is known to attract
"mavericks," men and women who tend to go their
own way.

Of course, being too hardheaded can be a substantial
roadblock to career success in any profession. Getting
ahead—along with many other attributes—demands a
strong sense of team play.

The maverick role of the DPer probably stems from
many things, but primarily from the mysterious
language that permeated the field in its earlier days,
and the complex technology that spawned a whole

world of people who understood it and could make it work—and who were content to keep its secrets to themselves.

But those days have changed. The computer has become part of most people's lives. It is no longer the domain of a select few. The personal computer has joined the television set, microwave oven, and stereo as a household staple, and while the average person has not developed an interest to match the professional DPer's, "bits," "bytes," and "baud rates" have become part of our public vocabulary. Which doesn't mean, by the way, that everyone understands what computers and data processing are all about. Recently, a man answered an ad we ran for a programmer position. He stressed in his résumé that he was experienced with programs—he'd worked at *Playbill,* which publishes theatrical *programs.* Obviously, he wasn't invited in for an interview. I suppose he is typical of a certain percentage of the population who would have difficulty telling a computer from a typewriter. Still, as we forge ahead into the computer age these people become more of a minority. The fact is, as we all know, it is not uncommon these days to find executives who have terminals and keyboards at their desks and households using terminals for a variety of tasks. The computer is part of us—and we are part of the computer age.

This means that the person forging a career in data processing can no longer fall back on being keeper of the technology and its inherent mysteries. In fact, success in data processing these days demands *exactly the opposite.* The technological expertise must be present, of course, but it is the application of the technology that counts in today's marketplace. The computer tail no longer wags the management dog, and the data processor who approaches a career with that understanding has already established the proper attitude for success in this field.

Let's go back to the "personality" of the data processor. Obviously, an interest in technical data—as well as the ability to digest it—is important for anyone in DP. This doesn't run contrary to my previous statement about not allowing the technological tail to dictate the end result. As with the accountancy example mentioned in my introduction to this book, technical knowledge and skill will always be needed to enter the field and to advance in it. What's important, however, is that the accountant who remains chained to facts and figures, and who never looks beyond the ledger sheet to its *meaning*, will always be in shackles.

The same holds true for the data processor. You're expected, of course, to know your technical "stuff." If you want to achieve management success, you'll be expected to retain that technical knowledge while at the same time looking beyond the computer terminal to what end your technical input achieves.

Two professors from the University of Colorado, J. Daniel Couger and Robert Zawacki, have written a book titled *Motivating and Managing Computer Personnel*. They based a large portion of the book on a study of the needs of men and women in the data-processing field and how they are motivated to fill those needs in a job setting.

The study looked at three specific areas:

1. Social Need Strength (SNS).
2. Growth Need Strength (GNS).
3. Motivation Potential Score (MPS).

The SNS delved into how much social interaction the average DPer needs in order to be happy on the job. Because many in the field, or at least those who entered it early, seem to prefer to interact more with their machines than with their peers, it was expected that the score in this area would be low. But no one, including the researchers, expected it to be quite *so low*. In fact, people in data processing had the lowest SNS scores of six hundred professions included in the study.

At the same time, the GNS—Growth Need Strength—scores were the highest of those six hundred professions.

The MPS scores for motivational potential were generally high for DPers.

The conclusion? DP people want the potentials of career growth and most likely see their chosen field as being able to provide it.

But here's where that SNS—Social Need Strength—rears its ugly head, at least from my perspective as someone deeply involved in the world of career achievement and success. The tendency to shun interpersonal relations on the job, and to depend upon introspective interaction with the technology in front of you, is counterproductive to achieving success beyond the computer.

Let me quickly say that I am not being critical of those who prefer to avoid the broader scope of daily business life. Every industry needs people who are content to do that, and who achieve satisfaction and rewards from focusing on their technical tasks. In fact, those working in data processing bring to the workplace an interesting and challenging *new* set of needs for management to grapple with in the coming years. People involved in technically innovative jobs don't respond as readily as nontechnical managers to such incentives as raises, security, hours, job titles, and location, according to various studies. The opportunity to learn new skills and to be left to function freely on interesting projects ranks higher.

For those of you who are looking for advancement within the technical scope of data processing, the rules for success differ somewhat from a quest for promotions to more general, nontechnical management positions. The differences are not, however, as profound as the similarities.

Most people in every walk of life have difficulty taking stock of themselves, particularly when it involves acknowledging weaknesses. This is often why individuals end up in jobs—and careers—in which they're unhappy and unfulfilled.

Let's take the example of a programmer who fits the psychological profile in the book by Couger and Zawacki. For reasons that have little to do with job fulfillment—family pressure, or chasing the myth that success is measured by the size of the office, the size of the salary and stock options, and the size of the title—

this person makes the shift from data-processing professional to a more general and nontechnical position in management. The myth is fulfilled, but the person spends his or her days missing what had once brought pleasure—being knee-deep in the technology of data processing. It's the old "Peter Principle" at work, being elevated to one's level of incompetence—or at least lack of interest.

This person would be better off looking for advancement *within* data processing.

On the other hand, someone who doesn't fit the profile of the "average" DPer might be insuring the same level of unhappiness by *not* looking to use the data-processing experience and knowledge as a basis for seeking a more broad-based management position.

The point is that the adage "Know thyself" is an important first step in planning for success.

What other attributes are commonly applied to people working in data processing?

My own Burke Marketing studies in this area have turned up other personality traits (I might as well call them that) that seem to apply to a majority of people in data processing, at least according to the consensus of data-processing management, as well as top management from among the nation's one thousand largest corporations.

For instance, when asked why people in data processing *fail* to get ahead, lack of motivation led the list, with certain personal traits not far behind. The findings about motivation go hand-in-hand with Couger and Zawacki's conclusions. Data processors need motivation on the job. When it is absent, a lethargy sets in that is counterproductive to career advancement.

The personal traits pinpointed in the Burke study included an inability or unwillingness to get along with others in the corporation; an inability to communicate clearly; a lack of personality; and not being a good listener.

When those same respondents in a subsequent survey were asked to list the most important attributes of a good data processor, they put personal attributes higher than skills and abilities.

But let's go a step further. One of my studies strongly indicates that the three most important attributes when hiring a data processor are prior experience, technical know-how, and education.

Let's analyze these findings. It isn't difficult. *Getting* the job depends more upon data-processing skill. Advancing within the field (and outside it) demands much greater interpersonal skills to go along with the technical knowledge that nailed down the job in the first place.

Let's look at one other survey involving data processors. When asked whether, in general, data processors tend to be poor communicators, 60 percent of DP managers, and 70 percent of top management, said "Yes!"

None of this is surprising if the commonly held perception of data processors stands up. What's important about it from my vantage point is that the men and women who have entered the data-processing field obviously possess the technical knowledge, skills, and background to get the job—but will have to develop other skills and attitudes if solid career success is to be in their future.

As I said earlier, there are rules for success that apply to every career, no matter what the industry or profession, and there are those rules that are unique to data processing. Based upon the above-mentioned survey results, we've come up with one of the *success constants* that apply to DPers and to every other person with technical skills.

The person aspiring to career growth must adopt a broader outlook that sees beyond technical knowledge and skill.

2

THE FOUNDATION IS EDUCATION

Informal education that continues is better than formal education that ends at graduation.

Obviously, there are two levels of interest in a book like this—people already employed in data processing at all levels are looking to advance, and entry-level people are seeking their first jobs in the field. While this chapter is devoted to the latter, the principles involved have direct applicability to everyone, novice and veteran alike.

Those of you already working in data processing possess the requisite education (formal or otherwise) that got you your first DP job. Referring again to one of the Burke Marketing studies in Chapter 1, the three most important attributes in hiring a data processor are prior experience, technical know-how, and education. Certainly, at least a basic grounding in data-processing skills through some educational process is expected by companies looking to hire entry-level staff. But the fact that those of you already in data processing have achieved that educational level doesn't mean it ends there, particularly in an industry that changes so rapidly because of emerging technology. The concept of continuous education—of viewing one's life and career as a continuous learning process—is necessary for sustained career growth. There will be more about adding layers of education throughout a career later in this chapter.

For now, let's concentrate on the type of education necessary for someone looking for a first job in data processing.

The educational opportunities for computer study have grown with the burgeoning demand for people trained in this high-tech field. This presents a classic good news–bad news scenario. More education is available, but the quality of much of it has deteriorated. That's why it is imperative that once you have decided on a particular area of data processing to pursue, you do a thorough search for the right kind of training. The decision you finally make will be based upon a number of factors, including knowing yourself. A word of caution, however—what may be appealing to you today may change as you mature and as you spend more time in the field. I've seen numerous cases of men and women in every industry who set their sights too low in the beginning and then, once the promise of a broader and brighter horizon became evident, had to spend an inordinate amount of time making up for the deficiencies in their education. I recommend not only that you pursue the best possible data-processing training available to you—taking into consideration your financial and geographic limitations—but that you also shoot as high as possible in order to prepare yourself for the future twists and turns that occur in virtually every life.

Four-Year College Degree Programs

There has been a proliferation of data-processing degree programs in colleges and universities. The differences between them in quality and scope are as many as the names given the degree. A recent study indicated that more than two hundred colleges and universities use a different name for their introductory computer course, even though the course material is virtually identical at all the schools.

Basically, universities offer four-year degrees in two general areas of computer science—scientific programming, computer hardware, and software design; and business data processing. There are schools that try to combine both, but these are the exception rather than the rule.

This poses a dilemma for the incoming freshman with sights on a career in data processing. Which of the two basic courses of study do you choose? It might not be such a crucial decision if it were easy to shift from one school to the other, but curriculum requirements at many colleges and universities often preclude this to the extent that a switch in emphasis could tack an additional year onto your undergraduate schooling.

Once you have decided which area of data processing

is for you—and you have decided to take the four-year college route for your training (as opposed to two-year community colleges, private technical schools, and other avenues that are discussed later in this chapter)—you can begin evaluating each school's ability to properly prepare you for a career in DP. Clearly, all schools are not the same, particularly when it involves so highly technical a field as data processing.

First, of course, you should ascertain the qualifications of the faculty that will be teaching you computer sciences. What's more important here is the willingness on the part of faculty members to keep abreast of current concepts and to constantly upgrade and revise the material they teach. This is not a discipline in which a course plan developed five years ago will have much relevancy for today's student. Professors of Elizabethan English, zoology, and romance languages generally can teach what they learned twenty years ago with confidence and success to students today. Not so with a dynamic and rapidly changing field like data processing. New languages, new software programs, new hardware and applications demand that today's teacher of data processing be deeply involved in the changes in the subject matter. If you get the impression that the faculty of a college or university you are considering is likely to deal with computer science as in "the good old days," it's time to look at another institution.

If you are someone who has made the determination that scientific programming and computer hardware and software design are to your liking, take the time and trouble to assure yourself that you will be offered state-of-the-art technology that includes courses in data base, telecommunications, computer architecture, FORTRAN, Assembler (mini-micro), and Pascal languages, as well as other things that might not only be of particular interest to you, but reflect what is used in industry in your geographical area.

If your interest lies in the nuts and bolts of hardware, you might find computer engineering to be the right degree program for you. A number of colleges and universities now offer a degree in this area of computer science. This course of study obviously prepares the student for a number of jobs in data processing's most technical aspects, including such esoteric applications as robotics.

Management Information Systems (MIS)

This course of study often falls in the crack between hardware-software and more business-oriented computer curriculums. Some universities offer it in their school of business data processing, while others include it in their programming and more technically oriented schools. The basic difference is that students coming out of this academic discipline are usually more interested (and prepared) in the end use of data processing, rather than in the nuts and bolts of the machinery. That isn't to say that anyone involved in business applications of DP shouldn't have a firm grounding in the technical aspects of the equipment that makes all end use possible, but it's a matter of emphasis. One of the most important and developing specialties within data processing is MIS, and it is a good choice for those who love and understand computers and who set their sights on broader applications.

Business Data Processing

The actual degree offered by universities in this area of study varies from school to school. You might graduate with a Bachelor of Professional Administration, a Bachelor of Administrative Science, or a Bachelor of Administrative Management. It's all nomenclature and semantics. Like Management Information Systems, this pursuit prepares the graduating student for a more general end-use application of the training, rather than just the manipulation of equipment and systems. Professionals with whom I've spoken urge that those considering entering this four-year field of study make sure that they will be trained in at least three computer languages, with advanced classes in two of them. Languages most often suggested are COBOL, RPGII, and BAL. Other courses that should be included are systems analysis, fundamentals of data base and telecommunications, business management, and as many accounting courses as fit comfortably in the schedule.

It's always amazing to me how people are willing to enter into jobs or universities without taking the time to analyze whether the company or the college is right for them. I suppose it has to do with the buyer-seller relationship; in both cases, the individual is being accepted by management or admissions people and does not feel worthy to make judgments of such institutions. In some cases, of course, money and geography will determine what colleges are reasonably available to the student, but if there is an opportunity to compare colleges, I urge you to do so.

Here are some questions you might ask before making a decision:

• *Ask the college administration* what computers are available for hands-on use. Make your own tour to ascertain that the answer is accurate.

Try to determine to what degree the data-processing department is keeping up with the state of the art. Look for an abundance of technical manuals and trade journals. Chat with the teaching staff, and formulate some questions to lead them into a discussion of what continuing involvement they have with the field.

The fact that a data-processing department at a university is filled with exotic equipment doesn't necessarily mean that you'll have unlimited access to it. Determine what restrictions are placed upon student use.

Talk with one of the guidance counselors and make sure that the scheduling of courses will not make it unduly difficult for you to take all those that you feel are necessary.

The back of virtually every college admissions brochure contains a list of faculty and their credentials.

While a healthy smattering of advanced-degree teachers is good, you might also pay particular attention to any professional and business credentials faculty members possess. Computer science taught from a purely academic perspective often falls short in preparing a student for the practical realities of a data-processing career.

Randy Pace and Warner Coffman, data-processing specialists in our St. Louis franchise, add another reason to seek out a school in which at least a good number of the professors are connected with industry. Not only does it promise a more up-to-date approach to teaching data processing, but it puts you in touch with people who have connections with businesses in your area. Get to know these professors; they could become a good source of job leads upon graduation.

• *Ask other students* any questions that will enable you to judge the reliability of the answers you've received from faculty members and staff. I don't mean to imply that university officials would be deliberately dishonest with a potential student. It's just that a faculty's perception of a university's facilities and procedures is often different from that of its student body.

• *Ask graduates of the school* whether they thought that the training they received and their degree from that particular school were helpful to them in entering the data-processing industry and in helping them achieve career growth in it.

Ask especially about the placement office at the university. Does its staff really make an attempt to place students in industry, or is it more of a counseling service that results in few actual placements? But remember, finding a good job will, in all probability, be your responsibility.

Finally, even though their education was good enough to get them a job, did it give them sufficient knowledge to *succeed* in their first job?

• *Ask local industry* how many graduates of the university you're considering attending have been hired. Try to get some candid evaluation of how local industry leaders view the training of graduates from that university.

I don't mean to suggest that you should limit yourself to these questions. What I do hope to get across is a sense that the decision you make regarding a four-year college involves exactly that—four years out of your life, four years in which your future in your chosen career will be substantially determined. There are fields in which the simple possession of a degree almost insures at least some initial success in entering the field. Not so with data processing. The quality of your education, while perhaps not so crucial a factor in finding your first job, will play an increasingly important role as you progress in your career. I'm not referring to "college ties," although certain professions tend to select job candidates from certain schools. The Harvard Law School network is well known, as is the network of graduates of such engineering schools as the Massachusetts Institute of Technology and Rensselaer Polytechnic Institute. For most of us, however, choosing a school because of a certain ring to its name does little to determine what kind of success we'll have in the future. That is much more dependent upon the individual's initiative and desire (as well as prudent career moves) than upon a degree from a prestigious university.

But those four years provide the educational foundation for everything you will do in the future, and to enter into such a prolonged course of study without doing your homework is, at best, not very smart.

Community and Junior Colleges

These schools fill a vital need in communities across America and for the most part do an excellent job of providing a different educational path for students to choose. This is especially true in computer sciences. Two-year schools often provide better training for fledgling DPers than their four-year counterparts. There is more of a focus on the practical, rather than on the theoretical, which makes sense. Students complete a course of study at most of these schools in two years, and some schools offer certificates for periods as short as six and nine months. More knowledge has to be crammed into less time when compared to four-year institutions.

One of the strengths of community and junior colleges is their flexibility. The administrators of these schools are not so bound up in bureaucratic red tape and tradition when it comes to modifying course material. This enables them to shift with the changes in data processing, which, as I said earlier, is important.

There are basically two approaches the aspiring data processor can take with these schools.

The first is a two-year program that usually leads to an Associate's Degree. Under such a plan, students take not only a full range of required computer-related studies, but also an array of liberal arts courses that provide a much-needed balance to the more technical aspects of data-processing education.

Students coming out of a two-year study are prepared for a variety of entry-level data-processing jobs and will have had enough grounding in the broad area of computer sciences to take on some advanced and challenging positions.

The shorter curriculums, usually six to nine months and culminating in a certificate, are naturally more limited. Still, with the right kind of faculty and equipment and, most important, an educational philosophy that adjusts to changes in the field of data processing, these certificates enable a student to seek, with confidence, such entry-level DP jobs as data entry, assistant programmer, word processor, and computer maintenance technician.

Naturally, the same questions should be asked of a community or junior college that you'd ask of a four-year university before deciding to enroll.

Technical Trade Schools

In a sense, these schools, of which there are more than seven thousand, aim to prepare their students for careers in data processing in much the same way community and junior colleges do. The student body of each is made up of men and women who are looking to enter the work force faster than their four-year college and university counterparts.

But there are differences. A trade school focuses exclusively on the technical aspects of data processing. If that's your bent, these schools can do a good job of preparing you. What they fail to offer, of course, is a broader educational atmosphere in which liberal arts and other nontechnical courses can be taken.

Technical trade schools for data processing run the gamut from excellent to deplorable. The good ones have some sort of accreditation. The best are generally associated with the National Association of Trade and Technical Schools (NATTS). This organization is located in Washington, D.C., and it makes sense to contact it before deciding on a school. NATTS offers a variety of booklets and listings that can make your decision easier, to say nothing of making it productive.

One thing to be wary of is the trade school that makes unrealistic promises about job placement. Do your homework just as you would for four-year institutions and community colleges. Most important, begin to develop the attitude that finding a job in data processing, and forging a career in it, is your responsibility, not a placement office's responsibility. While you're learning data processing, be constantly on the lookout for job opportunities. Seek out part-time jobs to supplement your training. Often, such a part-time job turns full-time after graduation.

*   *   *

These are the major avenues of education for someone wanting to enter the data-processing field. There are others—for example, the armed forces provide an extensive and excellent array of training opportunities in all phases of data processing. Like trade schools—and because they are training people to perform tasks—they focus on technology to the exclusion of other academic areas. They also pay their "students" to learn.

Most communities offer some form of data-processing training through adult education courses at local schools. These can provide someone working in another field but wishing to enter data processing with an introduction to the knowledge necessary to make the switch. Even if you have no ambition to become a data processor, but realize, as everyone does these days, the need to have some familiarity with computers, these adult education courses offer an inexpensive and convenient way to pick up that knowledge.

Finally, there is home study. This is the least effective means of preparing yourself for a career in data processing, but again, much depends upon the individual's motivation and desire to succeed. A highly motivated person can get more out of a home-study course than a lazy, uninspired individual taking up expensive chair space at a top university.

Those are the choices. Interestingly enough, the opportunities available in data processing—and the unusual demands it makes—have created an educational situation that runs contrary to patterns associated with other fields, especially in light of some of the studies I've already mentioned.

Technical knowledge is a requisite for entry into data processing, according to my Burke study. But it's the "softer" knowledge—the ability to communicate, to understand the broader business ramifications of data processing, the vision that goes beyond the computer terminal—that determines *real* success over the long haul. That's why there is an emerging trend for those wanting a career in data processing *not* to study it in the undergraduate university setting. Generally, the educational flow has been for students attending a two-year community or junior college to move from there into a four-year institution where their credits can be applied toward a degree. With data processing, the opposite approach might make more sense. For one thing, technical knowledge absorbed toward the end of one's educational process has a better chance of sticking.

But there's another reason.

It is dramatically more difficult for an individual to become a well-rounded, *educated* person. Developing the communications skills (written and verbal English) and an understanding of global business (finance, accounting, political science, negotiating techniques, languages), social issues (psychology, sociology, history, literature), and other disciplines necessary for continued growth in *any* field is more difficult than learning the technical aspects of data processing.

I can hear the moans now. It sounds as though I'm downplaying technical education for the data processor. Far from it. What I am suggesting is that data processors—like accountants, engineers, scientists, and all other technically based professionals—benefit from being able to communicate their technical knowledge and skills.

A number of years ago, Purdue University, a fine institution specializing in engineering, became aware that its graduates, as a whole, did not advance as quickly up the corporate ladder as did graduates from other good engineering schools. Purdue's engineering training was as good as that offered by other institutions. Why, then, was advancement slower?

The answer Purdue came up with was that while its engineering graduates were as technically skilled as their counterparts from other schools, those other institutions had insisted that students take more courses in written and oral communications.

It makes sense. A person can be filled with information, but if that information isn't being effectively communicated to fellow workers and to top management, it remains solely within that individual. It again comes down to viewing technology and knowledge of it as being valuable only to the extent that it contributes to a larger goal. For that to happen, communication must take place.

Doctors are another example of this. Medical schools are slowly but surely integrating courses in the humanities into the medical curriculum. It has to do with social pressure and, because we have become a litigious society, an attempt to lower the risk of malpractice actions against physicians. A recent study indicated that physicians with a pleasant personality and sense of "the human condition" are less likely to be sued for malpractice. Students entering medical school have been chosen, for the most part, because of their academic records involving "hard sciences." Yet when they become physicians they find themselves dealing with human beings, not just scientific theory, and too many of them are unable to bridge the gap.

The same holds true for data processors. Having a firm grasp of a complex system is one thing; conveying data and information to end users in comprehensible, nontechnical language is another.

That is why acquiring a more liberal and well-rounded education *before* specializing in technical aspects of data processing is an attractive approach to some students with their sights set on a data-processing career. It certainly is not for everyone. In fact, it probably is not the approach most men and women should take as they begin preparations for a career in the field. But there is a certain wisdom to it, and as you progress through this book that wisdom will become more apparent, especially for those of you looking to use data processing as a springboard into the world of management.

3

KNOWING HOW TO GET A JOB

Finding a good job is a job and a half.

It doesn't matter whether you've just come out of college and are looking for your first job in data processing or are an experienced programming analyst or systems supervisor looking to advance to higher positions in the field. The résumés might be different, but the task of finding a job involves basic rules that apply to everyone. What follows in this chapter is a step-by-step formula for going after a data-processing job.

Let's begin with a basic rule, one that too many people choose to ignore: looking for a job *is a job and a half.* It demands the same attention to detail, the same hard work, and the same management requisites as working full time in a data-processing position.

In this case, you're managing *you!* You're the company, and how well you manage it will determine whether "its stockholders"—you—will see the stock pay big dividends over the years.

Getting Started

Having a Plan

You'd think that after more than thirty-five years of finding people jobs, I would long ago have ceased to be amazed at how many people approach job hunting like a lottery—they buy a ticket (a degree, a certificate, experience) and wait to see if their number is called. Countless talented and educated men and women fail in their chosen professions because they adopt a helter-skelter, passive philosophy, and when jobs fail to materialize, they chalk it up to "fate" or claim that the only way to get a job is to "know someone" or to "be in the right place at the right time."

No one would deny that jobs sometimes do materialize because of timing, or because we know someone who happens to be aware of an opening that's right for us. But even then, knowing such a person often is the result of working hard at building a *network* of friends and contacts within a field. It isn't luck that you knew the right person at the right time; give yourself more credit than that.

I recently spoke before a New York University graduate school alumni group. After I finished my success-oriented talk, a man approached me and asked if he could have a few minutes of my time. He gave me a thumbnail sketch of his background, which was quite impressive. He then told me that because he'd spent the last two years working overseas, he didn't have any contacts.

I must have looked startled, because he quickly added, "Well, hardly any."

I said, "Those few you do have can direct you to others, if you use the networking approach, and those others can direct you to even more people." I then asked him, "How well do you know the dean here?"

"I know him pretty well," he said.

My response was, "Other than administrative and management functions, what do deans generally do?"

He replied, "They're goodwill ambassadors and make every effort to generate money for the university."

"Right," I said, "and they have a tremendous number of contacts with influential businesspeople. Why don't you start right now and ask the dean for a half-hour appointment in the near future? That way, you'll have begun your networking tonight, right here."

He thanked me and said, "You've got me thinking. I just thought of some executives who might be helpful."

The point is that contacts are out there—you just have to think logically about who they are and how to get to them.

When a company is formed and sets out to succeed, it drafts a plan in which it focuses on its strengths, the sector of its overall industry in which it wishes to position itself, the competition it is likely to face, and countless other factors. A company that simply opens its doors without such a business plan is generally doomed to failure.

An individual looking for a job should do the same thing: devote enough time to thinking and research *before* beginning the *business* of job hunting.

Getting Organized

Before developing such a plan, you must recognize the need to be organized. If you have lived your entire life keeping important names, addresses, phone numbers, and other bits of information scribbled on the backs of envelopes and on matchbook covers, you might want to consider becoming more *formally organized*. In fact, it's a necessity, not only for a particular job search but as a habit that will benefit you throughout your career. Being disorganized has never impressed a boss who's looking for something from you in a hurry, or a prospective employer who wasn't called back on time because you used up all the matches and tossed away the matchbook.

The *place* in which you work is important. So is the place from which you're conducting your job search. If you're already employed and thinking of leaving, your present office might serve, but be careful. If you haven't resigned yet and are using the company's time, supplies, and telephone to look for a job, you're almost insuring an angry boss and a bad reference. If that practical ramification doesn't faze you, consider the unfairness of it. Of course, if you have resigned and have asked for and received permission to use your office to look for another job, that's fine. The same goes if you have been fired. Many firms, recognizing the difficult position they have put an employee in, will be more than generous in allowing the dismissed person to use the office as a base of operations. If this is your situation, graciously accept the offer and utilize it, being careful, of course, not to overstep your bounds.

If you are looking for a new job and don't have the use of your former office, or if you are looking for your first job in data processing and must operate from home, creating an office atmosphere is helpful and productive. Again, let me stress that looking for a job *is a job and a half*. To view it as less than that is to cheat yourself of needed support systems.

Here are some things you can do to create the sense of being "on the job" when you're looking for a job.

First, find a space in your home that is conducive to establishing a work environment. That sometimes is difficult in cramped quarters shared with others, but it can be done. It takes planning, a heart-to-heart talk with those with whom you share the space, and the willingness to spend a little money to optimize the space.

A telephone is the next important item. Here's where you might have to spend some extra money, depending on your circumstances. Will others sharing your space tie up the phone for an inordinate amount of time? I wonder how many job opportunities have been lost when an employer, eager to hire someone, couldn't get through because teenagers were engaged in hour-long conversations with friends. If that's the situation in your household (and you can't talk reason to your own children), consider ordering a second line with a number that is to be used *only by you*.

The point is, once again, to consider your quest for a job every bit as important as a business wanting open lines of communication to prospective customers. After all, those prospective employers out there are your customers. If they can't reach you, they'll buy (hire) elsewhere.

What else do you need?

Perhaps an answering service or machine. Services have certain advantages—they are retained on a month-to-month basis, which means that you can dispense with them once a job comes through. The disadvantages are that they can become so swamped with calls that they are slow to answer your calls, or in some cases don't answer at all. Another disadvantage is that you lose control of the message given to a caller.

An answering machine solves those problems. You determine exactly what message is given (and the tone in which it is given), and you can program a machine to answer on the first or second ring (which I recommend).

The disadvantage of an answering machine is that it involves an initial investment. You can't cancel it as you would an answering service. Still, today's answering machines come at all prices, and a dependable one can be bought for a relatively small amount of money.

A thought about the greeting you record on an answering machine: if you tend to have a brusque telephone manner, or sound uncomfortable in a recorded message, get someone else to record it for you. And don't be cute. New answering-machine owners seem to enjoy the exercise of creative license—impersonating a movie star, using music behind the announcement, writing silly prose to get across the simple message that they aren't available and will call back. Avoid the temptation. Keep it simple: "This is John

Jones. I'm unable to take your call now, but if you'll please leave your name and phone number and a brief message following the beep, I'll get back to you as soon as possible."

How you establish the proper environment for your job search depends a great deal on you and on your work habits. The important thing is to attack the task of job hunting with the same resolve and sense of organization that you applied in your previous job. If it's a first job you are going after, it's a good opportunity to create good work habits that will carry over once you have landed something.

Looking for a job *is a job and a half.*

Viewing it that way will help make your search more productive and successful.

Targeting the Job You Want

If you are entering the field for the first time, the scope of your job search will possibly be broader than if you have already spent a few, or many, years in data processing and have had a chance to experience various areas of it and focus your thinking. Still, even for the neophyte, it pays to learn all you can about the field and its areas of specialization, and to analyze your strengths and interests as to how they might apply to specific job possibilities. The same holds true for deciding on the type of company with which you would be most comfortable, taking into consideration such variables as goegraphic location, company size, "corporate culture" (more on that later), and a host of other tangible and intangible factors.

For instance—and this is oversimplified—if you are committed to staying in a certain geographical area, there's no sense applying to corporations that will ask you to relocate. The same sort of narrowing down (and again, it's a matter of having taken the time and trouble to know who you are) applies if you want to stick with the purely technical end of data processing and are not interested in playing the "corporate game." If this is you, a smaller, high-tech company might offer you the most satisfaction in the long run. (On the other hand, working in smaller firms sometimes requires you to wear more than one hat, which can plop you smack dab in the middle of more management activity than in a larger corporation, where you can hide.)

If you wish to use your computer knowledge as a steppingstone to broader aspects of business, a large corporation with multiple divisions may offer more opportunity.

One strategy followed by thousands of young people entering a profession is to look for a first, and second and perhaps even third, job with a "springboard company." Every industry has them; some obvious ones are Xerox, Marriott, Procter & Gamble, R. H. Macy, and, of course, IBM. The springboard companies know that your eventual goal is to use their training and reputation to get you a top spot with a smaller firm. The result is that they offer impressive and generous incentives to keep the good ones, which, of course, is to your benefit even if you don't find that dream job outside IBM or Xerox.

Are there drawbacks to approaching your DP career this way? There are, if you're the sort of individual who has trouble functioning in a large corporate environment. If that's the case, your talents just won't shine. Also, opportunities at the top are highly limited, a problem if you decide to stay and seek higher positions within a large company. Again, it comes down to taking stock of your personality, abilities, and goals. If they match up with the springboard approach, consider it.

It might seem axiomatic that since you're trained in data processing, data processing *is your occupation*. That's too simple. The field has grown so that it encompasses a wide variety of occupations. The young man or woman seeking a first job in the field might be excused for viewing it as just that—one large occupation in which to get started—and might actually find that view more productive. Being open to a wide variety of first-job opportunities makes sense. You might have your goals set on a particular specialty in data processing, but exposure to different areas will open up broader vistas.

For the experienced DPer, chances are you have had exposure to various subspecialties in data processing and are looking to advance in the one that makes the best use of your background and, simultaneously, will give you the greatest psychic and monetary rewards.

It has been my experience, and the experience of many data-processing specialists, that too many DPers, especially first-time job seekers, adopt a narrow view of what jobs to pursue. Being open, especially at the start of a career, gives you greater latitude and increases your potential. Naturally, the specific training you have received will help determine which jobs are available to you, but it doesn't stop there. Good companies look for qualities in people that transcend specific education and technical skills. Willingness to explore a variety of challenges within the broad field of data processing is appealing to a prospective employer.

I'm not suggesting that you shouldn't set your sights on some specific goal, especially in the future. Everyone benefits from looking ahead and determining where they would like to be in their careers ten and twenty years later. The trick is to be not so rigidly bound to that goal that opportunities aren't recognized—and acted upon—along the way.

The same principle holds true, of course, for the experienced DPer looking for a new job within the field. Immersing yourself in a narrow specialty, and concentrating on, for instance, only one programming language or utilizing only a single hardware system, certainly makes you an "expert" in those things. It might also limit your overall career growth. If you are one of those people I mentioned earlier who are content to remain within a technical specialty and have no aspirations to broaden their base, you have reached your goal and should prosper in it. That's the sort of decision only you can make, after you "know thyself."

But for those who are not content to remain within a closely prescribed data-processing specialty, an open attitude toward all the possibilities and potentials of the field make sense.

Frank Goldschmidt, a data-processing specialist in

our Boston office, recently told me of a young man he had been dealing with who typified someone who sets a goal for the future and is willing to make a variety of moves in order to obtain the necessary experience and knowledge to reach it. This young man's objective was to become a systems programmer in an IBM MVS shop. He had the education, intelligence, and desire, but lacked the right "buzz words." His experience included only PL1 programming in an IBM DOS shop.

His first move was to take a PL1/COBOL job on the basis of his PL1 skill. Next, he went to a COBOL/OSVS1 shop based upon his COBOL skill. His next move was to ask for a vacant systems-programming slot. He got it, then was offered an MVS job on the basis of his systems-programming experience.

While this young man found it necessary to change companies to acquire skills, the same career progression can sometimes be achieved by seeking transfer within your own company.

The next question that should be pondered by the job seeker is the *industry* in which the work will be performed. This is an interesting area because, while some people put it first on their list of considerations, my research indicates that it should rank considerably lower than that. Job satisfaction, according to my studies, ranks much higher than does happiness with the field in which the job is performed. A good programmer, analyst, or MIS specialist will find happiness performing those tasks in *any* industry provided that everything is right about the job itself—salary, surroundings, challenges, and advancement opportunities. Based upon my experience, I would strongly suggest that the industry in which the data processor functions be considered less important than the job itself—provided, of course, that the industry isn't on a downward spiral. If it is, future potential might be limited.

Still, there are so-called glamor industries that hold out important psychological lures for certain individuals. Take the case of someone who has always wanted to be a rock-and-roll star but, because of the realities of earning a living and supporting a family, has also pursued an education in data processing. It might be important for that person to work as a programmer in some aspect of the music industry, even though the job itself might pay less and have to be performed in uncomfortable physical surroundings. There's little doubt that being interested in the end product of data processing—tracking record sales, let's say, instead of tracking the sales of nuts and bolts—can make a big difference in a person's mental attitude on the job and, by extension, affect that person's performance and career growth. If that's the case with you, it narrows down the jobs you will pursue. If it isn't—and your pleasure comes from the work you perform, rather than from the industry in which it is conducted—your horizons are broadened considerably.

My advice is to get your data-processing career started in almost *any industry*. Once you are launched and have amassed some solid background, you can begin investigating those industries in which your skills are needed, and that will afford you a greater measure of inner satisfaction.

Certain positions, such as data entry, are plentiful and relatively easy to land. But if that is not what you want, it is better to hold out even though it might prolong your job search. It takes a lot longer to rise from a data-entry position than it does from a programming or systems-analyst job. That's why the next item to be considered is the *position* within a company or within a particular data-processing department. The goal should be to start as high as possible within a company's management structure. Those who start higher tend to advance faster than those who start lower. I'm not suggesting that job applicants apply for positions that are beyond their training and capabilities, but I do believe in extending one's reach. Data processing presents a particularly difficult problem in this regard. The same job and responsibilities carry different titles at different companies. Still, the basic principle remains the same. Whatever job you are presently holding down says a great deal about you to a prospective employer. It's a reflection of the way you are viewed by your current employer, and it can determine the level of employment you might be considered for in a new company. I'm not talking about titles alone, although a title is important. It is more a matter of your attitude about yourself and about your worth as a professional data processor. Whether you are seeking another job within the field or are looking for your first job, it is important that you not lose sight of the goals you have established for yourself, and that you not jump at whatever is offered out of fear that it is "the only job in town." It may be, of course, at least for the moment, but to settle because of a lack of confidence in yourself can have a detrimental impact further along in your career.

There's something else to consider when deciding what sort of DP job to go after, and that is the possibility of turning any job you end up with into one that better suits you. I'm not talking about moving to another job within the company. I *am* talking about shaping the job you have into one that expands its original horizons. Here's that open-mindedness I mentioned earlier. Simply because the position you have taken has a detailed job description attached to it doesn't mean you can't alter that set of parameters as you go along. Naturally, you have to do a top-notch job in the area for which you were hired, but you can, at the same time, explore other areas of the company that might benefit from your skills and position. Making contacts outside of your immediate department can lead to this broadening of your role and ultimately increase your worth to the company. There is one potential drawback to this, however. If you become *too* successful at it, you might find yourself spread too thin and neglect your primary responsibilities. Also, when looking for a new job outside the company, you don't want to have your experience diluted to the extent that it confuses a potential employer. But I wouldn't let that relatively remote possibility cause you to clip your wings. Just make sure you keep tabs on yourself, and if you feel you have gone too far, pull back a little.

Obviously, every working man and woman has need for an *income* that will support a particular life style and personal obligations. Each person looking to enter the data-processing field, or to advance within it, should have a firm understanding of monetary needs and should be looking for a job whose salary range matches those needs. Here is where realism sets in, however. I've known too many people who set unrealistically high salary goals, considering the basic pay range within their occupation, and taking into account what they have to offer. On the other hand, there are people who set their sights too low. These individuals are usually dealing from a base of insecurity and feel that if they are paid less, their chances of being laid off or fired are lowered. Neither approach—going for pie-in-the-sky or undervaluing one's worth in the marketplace—makes sense. Some hard-nosed analysis of your training, ability, and experience, coupled with realistic knowledge and understanding of your career path, will enable you to more reasonably match up goals with opportunities.

The question of money is always a sticky one when going after a job. Naturally, the employer wants to hire a valuable new employee at the lower end of the salary range the occupation generally commands. You, the employee, would like a salary at the higher end of that range. During the job-interview phase you will be asking what the job pays and the employer will be asking how much you want. It is best to avoid answering the employer's question for as long as possible, parrying it with "Right now, the salary isn't uppermost in my mind. I'd prefer to find out the potentials of the job and of my role in the company."

The thinking behind this approach is that once you are the person the employer decides to hire, it's easier to ask for a higher salary. You're the one who's been chosen, and the employer is more likely to up the offer, rather than have to start interviewing other candidates again.

Randy Pace and Warner Coffman of our St. Louis franchise suggest that if you reach a salary impasse, and if you really want the job, you agree to accept the lower salary on the condition that you be reviewed in six months rather than twelve. It has been their experience, and the experience of many other data-processing specialists in other of my franchises, that this approach will often generate more long-term money than the difference represented between the salary that was offered and the salary the candidate was holding out for.

Where Are the Jobs?

There are basically two types of job seekers—those who go out and find jobs and those who sit back and wait for jobs to come to them. Needless to say, it is the first type who most often succeeds.

Remember, looking for a job is a job and a half, and that includes the tedious and often creative task of locating available openings. They don't materialize out of the blue, but they're there. There's a certain analogy between trout fishing and looking for a job. It isn't enough to be fully equipped with the right rod and reel and artificial flies. Once you have those things (for a job seeker they would include stationery, a telephone, a record-keeping system, and a properly written résumé), the trick is to know where the trout are, to seek out the deep pools in which the biggest and fattest are waiting to feed. For the fisherman, it means going beyond the obvious and putting yourself in the position of the fish. For the job seeker, it means the same thing: going beyond the obvious and using every ounce of your creative and intuitive powers to find the right job for you.

The first rule that I would recommend is that you be active. Psychotherapists have a favorite saying: "Any action is better than no action." It's a good philosophy and applies to many areas of life, including job hunting. Being active translates into being visible. The inactive job seeker remains below the surface, hoping that a "perfect" employer will come along and turn over the rock. That happens, but I certainly wouldn't bank on it.

You'll recall my earlier comments about people who chalk everything up to luck and to knowing the right person. These are very often the individuals who take the passive approach to job hunting and, because of that approach, experience undue difficulty in finding a first or new job in data processing. The fact is that you create your "luck"; you work hard to know the right people who can help you land a job. Fatalism is not a philosophy conducive to succeeding in job hunting, in business, or in life itself. Earthquakes will happen, but you can choose not to live on a fault. Floods will occur in the spring, but you can sandbag the banks before the water rises.

Being active, above all else, is crucial to your success as you seek a job in data processing.

How do you remain active while unemployed? It takes willpower, determination, tenacity, and commitment. Your daily routine should be no different while unemployed than it would be if you had to report to an office and put in a full day's work. And if you are employed and looking for a change at the same time, you have really got yourself a job and a half.

I recently met a young woman who was looking for a job in journalism. She'd been "looking" for four months without success. Her comment to me was, "Everybody wants to get into journalism. There just aren't any jobs out there."

I asked her how many letters she had written to publications that might be interested in hiring her. I was shocked at the response: she had solicited no more than a dozen publications, most of whom apparently did not even have suitable jobs available. I suggested that a dozen inquiries would represent one day's work, certainly not the cumulative effort of four months.

Companies engaged in mail-order business consider a 2 percent response to a mailing highly successful. The same attitude should be applied to job hunting. You don't need positive responses from the hundred companies to whom you send a letter and résumé. You need just one good one.

There are many ways to seek jobs, but the best, in my opinion, is to go back to former employers where you quit (under good conditions) and talk to them about rejoining the firm. In my company we have often rehired our alumni; it has always been a happy relationship for the employees and, I might add, for us as well.

An excellent approach is to use your network of contacts. There are others, of course, that should be simultaneously pursued—personnel recruiters and want ads—but nothing substitutes for utilizing people you already know and those you make contact with as part of your job-search procedure.

Networking basically involves two levels. The first is composed of those people already in your sphere of contacts, both personal and professional. Earlier, I spoke of a gentleman who had been overseas and therefore felt he did not have any contacts to call upon for employment in the United States. All it took for him was the realization that if he jogged his memory and creatively went over a list of the people he knew, he could come up with a long and helpful list of people to contact.

In your case, the same exercise can reap similar rewards. Is there anyone you know who might be in a position to hire you? Think hard about it. How about contacting your friends in DP who are at your level, or in jobs at higher or lower levels? More than likely, one of them will introduce you to an executive in their company. Have you thought of speaking to hardware and software salespeople? They get around and are often excellent sources. And what about those acquaintances you have met at meetings, conferences, and conventions? They can be a gold mine of solid leads.

Chances are someone will emerge if you put your mind to it. Yes, that would be ideal, but, unfortunately, that's the point where too many people stop in building and using a network. What's important is that every single person you contact is the potential source of another contact. The individual who would be in a position to hire you directly might not have any openings, but once you've talked to that person, other names might come up at other companies who could be potential sources of employment. Here again, this is where passivity gets you nowhere. Let's say you've come up with the name of someone you believe might be in a position to hire you. Call that person, introduce yourself, using the name of the person who recommended you, and indicate that you are interested in finding another job in data processing.

You should ask if you can set up an appointment to see the person with whom you are speaking. If you know there are jobs that you qualify for available with that company, you can be direct about wanting to be interviewed for one of them. If you sense or know that there aren't any openings at the moment, ask if you can come in for some advice and guidance. If either or both approaches fail, you then have a choice of simply saying "Thank you," or you can say "I appreciate your time, and I'd also appreciate any leads you can give me of other people in the industry with whom I could speak."

It pays to be as specific as possible. If there are a couple of companies in your area that you would be interested in working for, instead of simply asking for names from your original contact, you might say "I'd be interested in working for the XYZ Corporation. Is there anyone there you might put me in touch with?" The worst response would be "No, I don't know anyone, but if I think of someone I'll let you know." Then again, the response might be "Sure, Joe Smith and I are very active in the local Kiwanis. Joe's the manager of information services at XYZ. As a matter of fact, he was telling me the other day at lunch that they're expanding and . . ."

Nothing ventured, nothing gained. There are many adages to sum up that philosophy, but they all say the same thing, and they are all equally valid. Be direct, tell the person what you want, and begin developing a network of people who know you are available, who know you have the right credentials, and, hopefully, who know someone who can be of direct help to you.

I can't stress enough the need to be open and flexible. As with the fly fisherman who must go where the fish are, the job hunter must go where the jobs are. One word of caution if geography is particularly important to you: if you are, let's say, shooting for a job three years from now in western Michigan, take the time to study the market there so that you don't end up gaining three years' experience on systems and equipment not in vogue in western Michigan. I use that location as an example because Joe Grabinski, of the Robert Half Grand Rapids office, makes the point that if a programmer and/or analyst accumulates two years of COBOL and Manufacturing and/or CICS, he can almost guarantee that person a position in western Michigan. On the other hand, he says, "If they show up here with several years of NETA/3 or FORTRAN, I invariably have to say, 'Good luck!' "

It all comes back to doing your homework, whether it applies to a future geographical move or specific companies with whom you'd like to work. Professional magazine writers know that the biggest mistake they can make is to write an article or query for a magazine they haven't read. Each magazine has its own editorial style, and failing to research it is like shooting at targets in the dark. The same rule should apply to all job seekers, with perhaps an even greater need for it in the data-processing field. How embarrassing (and nonproductive) to gain an interview in a company you're high on and find that everything you're talking about has little or no application to that particular firm. Learn everything you possibly can about a company before approaching it for a job. Try to get hold of its annual reports. Use the library to research articles that might have been written about the company or authored by the people who'll be interviewing you. Do your homework; it pays off.

At this point I'd like to suggest a technique that seldom fails. I certainly don't recommend making blind calls to busy executives in the hope that one will agree to have you in for an interview. The process just doesn't work that way. A better approach, especially if you are young and seeking your first position in DP, is to call someone in the data-processing department of a company in your area, introduce yourself, indicate that you are looking to change jobs, or to get started in the field, and wonder if you could "get some advice from professionals like you." People are always flattered to be asked for advice. The fact that you are not asking for an interview and job takes the pressure off them. The worst that could happen is that you will be told they're too busy at the moment to accommodate you. If that occurs, you are then free to ask for some names of people at other companies who might not be under so much pressure and would be willing to give you a few minutes of their time. Here's how the network grows, one name leading to another and pyramiding until, before you know it, you have an extensive list of people who might be able to help. This same approach is as valid for the first-timer as it is for the veteran data processor. The veteran, of course, has had the advantage of having naturally built a network of contacts through daily activities in the workplace. At least, that's what should be done. Too often, people fail to keep track of the contacts they make within their field, and when it comes time to change jobs, most of those names are forgotten. I firmly believe that everyone, no matter what the occupation, should be contantly "interviewing" for a better job within their own company or be prepared, if necessary, to look elsewhere. This involves paying close attention to the *business* of being employed. I've written many articles on the subject of "insuring" one's career by doing precisely what the personnel department of a corporation does—keeping careful records of your contributions to the company, of your involvement with the industry on a broader level, and, in line with the concept of networking, of those people with whom you have interacted and upon whom you might call when it is time to look for greater and more lucrative challenges.

There are other aspects of insuring a career, which we will consider later in this book. For now, what's important is to recognize that your most valuable resource in looking for a job is other people, and if you neglect to take advantage of that resource, you significantly diminish your chances of finding the kind of employment you desire.

Temporary DP Work

If you happen to be out of work (it happens to the best of us, even in a growth industry like data processing), you'll have time on your hands, no matter how aggressively you are pursuing a job in data processing. That time can hang heavy unless you make productive use of it. One way of doing that is to take additional courses in other aspects of the field that you are not familiar with. This will broaden your base when a job does become available and you are in competition for it. The second productive use of time is to seek temporary employment. This accomplishes many things. First, of course, it generates income, which takes the pressure off you during your period of unemployment. The second benefit of doing temporary data-processing work is that it exposes you to a variety of DP situations that can accomplish the same end result as taking courses. The difference is that you are being paid to learn. The third, and certainly as important as the previous two, is that it puts you in touch with professionals in the field who might be in a position to hire you on a permanent basis. We've had countless examples of men and women who took temporary DP

jobs through our Accountemps service (which specializes in placing temporary professionals in the DP and
financial fields) and ended up being hired full time by
the company. It's not uncommon for management to be
so impressed with the job done by the temporary
worker that a permanent job actually is created in order
to keep that person on staff.

And then there is a group of DPers who do not prefer
permanent employment. They like to go from one assignment to another through temporary services like
Accountemps, or work for contract programming organizations. Again, it's a matter of attitude. Working in
the data-processing industry in *any* capacity makes
sense. The only word of caution I offer, if you genuinely
want a permanent job, is that you not become so busy
with temporary work that you no longer have time for
your main job—the job of finding a job.

Others in the Network

Let's say you have done a good job of searching your
memory for anyone and everyone who might be in a
direct position to help you land a good data-processing
job. So far it hasn't worked, but that doesn't mean you
should give up. In order to expand the network you
are creating, you should begin making contact with
virtually everyone you know, no matter how remote
you think they might be. Busy, successful people get
around, touching bases in many fields. Your family
lawyer might be a source: perhaps he represents a

data-processing company and could be in a good position to refer you to that firm. Your doctor might have a number of patients in that field, and if you happen to mention that you are looking for a new job, he could pass that on to a patient who comes in later in the day. If you have a relationship with a bank, the people in it might be a good source of job leads. Religious, fraternal, and political organizations are other possibilities. Of course, a natural source of leads would be professional organizations whose membership is composed of data processors. Check them out in your community. Some will have a job-referral service, not only for recent college graduates looking to enter the field but for experienced professionals who need help locating another position.

I use a messenger service on a regular basis. Messengers working for the firm come and go, but one young man has always impressed me. He is getting close to graduation from a local college and is working as a messenger to make ends meet. What impresses me about him is that his job takes him into a variety of business firms and he has made it a point, if he meets an executive, to work into the brief conversation that he is about to graduate and he would appreciate any advice that person might be able to give him. He is polite, bright, and sincere, and I have no doubt that some of the contacts in *his* network, generated through his use of a temporary messenger job, will pay dividends for him.

Good jobs and contacts usually don't come to the job seeker. It's up to the job seeker to cultivate contacts and make use of them. Those who fail to do that are tying their own hands.

Personnel Recruiters and "Headhunters"

One of my commissioned studies in the data-processing field asked what sources management used most for finding data-processing personnel. It was interesting to me that when we eliminated those respondents to the study who told our independent research firm that they did not know which source was the most important, recruiters and agencies ranked first. There's good reason for this, which I'll get into in a moment.

Finding jobs is big business, and the Yellow Pages has the names of those who specialize in the field.

The differences between them have little to do with what they call themselves—agencies, recruiters, search firms, or executive-placement specialists. They're all in the same business—matching available openings with job seekers. The employer pays the fee to the personnel recruiter or headhunter. It shouldn't come out of your pocket.

There are some basic rules you should apply when choosing a personnel-recruiting firm. Your instincts are, of course, your best barometer. You have to be comfortable with the person with whom you're dealing, and have faith in that person's professional ability. Stay away from services in which the people with whom you come in contact are basically high-pressure salespeople, rather than skilled professionals with a firm knowledge of the companies and industries in which they deal on a daily basis. Specialized services do a far better job than general-purpose services that try to be all things to all occupations and to all job candidates.

Check to see how long the service has been in business. It takes many years for them to develop the contacts, and for their clients to have faith in them. Those specialized services that have accomplished this are welcome when they submit a candidate for employment consideration. The company knows they have done their homework and have carefully evaluated and screened the people they send. Find a specialized service that pleases you—professional staff, years of experience in the data-processing field, a compatible placement person, and a realistic approach to your experience and job potentials. (The Robert Half organization, as an example, has been around almost forty years.)

Stay active. Be in touch with selected, specialized, personal recruiters, answer ads from the newspaper, make calls every day to build up your network of contacts, learn new facets of data processing, take some temporary assignments if you have the time, and work hard at the job of getting a job.

Want Ads

Answering newspaper want ads as a source of job leads is one of the more routine ways of seeking employment, and in many cases turns out to be productive. It doesn't, however—and shouldn't—take priority over contacting former employers and specialized personal recruiters. It's better to view it as an adjunct to your primary thrust.

There are a couple of things to keep in mind when using want ads.

The first is that once an ad hits the paper, it elicits many responses, which places you in a large field of candidates. In order to stand out from the crowd, your résumé and cover letter must be top-notch, designed to catch the eye of whoever does the initial reading of responses, in many cases a low-level staff member in the personnel department. (The section on résumés and cover letters, which appears later in this book, will provide you with helpful guidelines.)

Newspaper want ads should be answered promptly, certainly within the first week after the ad's appearance. Because you will probably be answering many ads at a time, it's important to set up a system to keep track of your replies and of any follow-up resulting from your response. The best technique is to clip the ads from the paper and attach them to individual file cards, with a notation on each of the date you responded. If your reply is answered, the names of the people with whom you speak, dates, times, and addresses and phone numbers should be noted on the card. Also, if you're using different versions of your résumé for different jobs (which I heartily recommend) be sure to note which version was submitted.

If it is a job for which you are specifically suited and it especially appeals to you, you might consider sending your reply by messenger or overnight courier service. It will get there quicker and, more important, it will stand out from the replies sent by conventional means.

If you haven't heard anything within a reasonable amount of time, make a phone call; if you replied to a blind ad, send a follow-up letter inquiring into whether your résumé and letter were received, and whether you are under consideration for the job. At worst, it might prompt a rejection, which will allow you to place that card in an inactive file, forget about *that* job, and get on to others.

A thought about "blind" ads—these are ads that do not indicate the name of the company offering the job. Be wary of these if you are employed and are looking for a new position. Your letter and résumé might end up on your current boss's desk, either because the job is with your present company or because a friend of your boss disclosed that you were looking for another job.

Reading, evaluating, and responding to want ads should definitely be a part of your job-search routine, and it should be pursued with diligence and order. Set aside sufficient time to do this work. It can't be sloughed off. *However* . . . keep in mind that most surveys and studies show that as many as *75 percent* of jobs are never advertised in the papers.

A few final thoughts on want ads:

Large companies take months to fill important jobs. Because an ad that appeared six weeks or two months ago no longer runs doesn't mean that the job has been filled. Don't hesitate to respond to those ads even after many weeks have passed. Assume nothing.

Get to know and understand what certain job descriptions and titles *really* mean. The myriad of job titles in data processing makes this especially important. Read enough want ads and the various usages of job titles in your area will begin to emerge.

Avoid ruling out jobs that appear in want ads because the required education, experience, and skills don't exactly match up with your own. If you're anywhere near the stated requirements, go after it. Many employers ask for loftier credentials than the job really requires, and readily settle for someone whose *real* qualifications match the job's *real* needs. Also, a want ad that calls for an unreasonable set of qualifications, but offers a salary that more accurately reflects a less demanding position, brings in fewer responses.

If you are willing to relocate, either subscribe to the best newspaper for employment advertising in the cities in which you are interested or have friends send you the help-wanted section of their city's Sunday edition. Be aware, however, that you may have to pay your own way to another city for an interview. Once you have decided to fly to, say, Los Angeles or New York for a specific interview, that's the time to launch a concerted letter-writing campaign to other firms there, specifying that you will be in the area and would appreciate seeing them while you are in town. This is a no-cost way for companies to get to interview talent from far away without having to pick up the tab, and the response you will receive might surprise you.

You can even consider placing a position-wanted newspaper ad in selected cities; either use a box number of the newspaper or pay for a service (usually through a telephone-answering service) that will forward written replies or phone messages to you if you have responses to your letter-writing campaign. In this way you will resemble a resident, which may encourage greater responses. Your present location will not be held against you if you are prepared to pay your relocation expenses.

4
PUTTING YOURSELF ON PAPER

A résumé will seldom get you a job offer.
A résumé will often lose you a job offer.

By and large, the worse résumés are from data processors. It constantly amazes me that people whose very occupation depends on accuracy, completeness, and detail so often produce résumés that are inaccurate, contain scanty information, and fail to spell out salient features of their background. A high percentage of DP candidates have no résumés at all and rely on services like ours to extract enough information from them to be able to market them to our clients. We don't mind providing that service, and we do it. The problem is that not enough thought to background is given by these job seekers. Most of what they say is off the top of their heads, and although we probe as best we can, the results may be incomplete. I don't have to remind DPers of the old acronym GIGO: "Garbage In, Garbage Out." This applies to résumés as well as to computer input.

And then there are some computer people who insist on preparing their résumés on a computer—often their company's computer. Would you hire a person who took the employer's time and supplies to look for another job? Besides, résumés call for conformity and readability. Make it easy for potential employers to find what they want, and, of course, spell out your achievements—that's what will get you a better job. Look at it this way: even when jobs are plentiful, the good ones are still hard to find. It's your career—make the best of it.

Résumés are perhaps the most bothersome aspect of job hunting. Maybe that's why so many of them are poorly done. These are the ones that are almost guaranteed to end up in the "Reject" basket—even if they have been written by the perfect candidate for a job opening.

I've been collecting material from résumés for many years. I call my files "Résumania," and have been doing a monthly column based on them for Dow Jones's *National Business Employment Weekly* for more than two years. The column is composed of the best (or worst) of real items taken from actual résumés. Every month, as I prepare the column, I am amazed at the ability of intelligent, educated, and experienced people to put their worst foot forward in an important aspect of gaining an interview for a job—their résumé.

The reason résumés seldom nail down a job for a candidate is that few people would hire someone sight unseen. Obviously, the personal interview, coupled with solid references, is the thing that brings about a tangible job offer.

But in order to reach the interview stage, the employer often has only one thing to go on (two, if you count the cover letter), and that's the written record of a person's past employment history and personal data. That's why it is imperative that you take the time to make sure that the résumé you send out to prospective employers is exactly what it should be—a clear, concise, visually attractive, and compelling presentation of someone the employer will want to meet and to interview.

For many people, the concept of writing anything is formidable. This is especially true of a data processor whose educational and professional focus has been on highly technical matters, not on becoming an efficient communicator, either verbally or with the written word. I indicated earlier in the book the need for data processors with an eye on higher management jobs to become better communicators. For now, the task at hand once you are ready to seek a new job is to write an effective résumé.

What should a résumé do?

It isn't enough to simply list a lot of data about yourself on a piece of paper. Sure, a factual presentation of your personal and professional life should be included, but if your résumé does only that—sum you up with facts and figures—you're going to be called in for significantly fewer interviews than you'd hoped for.

A résumé must hit the person reading it as having been prepared by someone of sufficient skills and *accomplishments* that *not* to call you in for an interview would be to risk losing just the right person for the job. That means that when preparing *your* résumé, you have to give considerable attention to making certain that it not only sums up your background but "sells" you as well. There are ways to do this, and one of the most important revolves around *accomplishments*.

To simply list job descriptions without indicating what accomplishments they represent is virtually to guarantee a cursory, uninterested reading by a prospective employer.

For example, a typical résumé will include the fact that you have spent two years as an office-automation analyst for XYZ Corporation. Chances are you would include the fact that this position involved the evaluation and implementation of word-processing and office teleprocessing hardware to provide data access to all levels of management.

Fair enough, but a simple statement of that does not indicate whether you were particularly good at it. What that particular item on your résumé should also include is the fact that during your two years with XYZ you analyzed data-access needs, proposed improvements to the system that would speed access at a lower cost, and eventually implemented a new system that not only accomplished its goals (faster access at lower cost) but won you an award from the Society of Office Automation Analysts. I'm being hypothetical, of course, but this a vital point.

I can hear it now: "That's fine for someone who's been lucky enough to do something like that in their previous job, but I really don't have any accomplishments to include. I did my job, that's all."

Few of us spend as much as two years at a job without accomplishing something worthwhile, and what it takes is the time and effort to go back over those years and recognize the contributions you made to your company. Of course, it's a lot easier if you have made note of them as they happened. You should keep an up-to-date personnel file on yourself, and that includes making note of each significant contribution you made at your company. Having this information at your fingertips is extremely helpful when it comes time to ask for a raise, and it has the same value when it comes time to prepare a résumé.

What have you accomplished in your previous employment that will cause a prospective employer to pull your résumé out of a file of hundreds, pick up the phone, and ask you to come in for an interview? That's what you must think about and work toward before you actually put your résumé together. Again, organization helps here. Take each job you've had, list it on a separate piece of paper, and reflect on your accomplishments for each, making notes as you go. Don't worry about creating too long a list. The important thing is to have that information in front of you when you actually describe that job on your résumé.

But before I get into the physical requirements of a good résumé, let's talk some more about the attitude that should be behind its creation.

If you aren't committed to turning out a letter-perfect résumé—every word spelled correctly, proper punctuation in place, sentences that are crystal clear and have been stripped of excess verbiage, attractive layout so that there is enough white space to make the page readable, and typed with an eye toward perfection, preferably by a professional typist—you may be better off not even bothering to produce and send a résumé to a prospective employer. While perfectly produced résumés seldom get someone a job, sloppy résumés can do a remarkably good job of making sure you'll never see the inside of an interviewer's office.

Think about the impression a carelessly prepared résumé has on the person receiving it. The employer realizes that of all the facets of someone's search for a job, the résumé is the one tool over which the applicant has total control. The job seeker can take as much time as necessary to think out clearly the way the résumé will be constructed and worded, and has control over the quality of its preparation. If something is wrong with it, such as bad spelling and punctuation, or inattention to its visual impact and ease of reading, it says that the individual really doesn't care very much. At the least, it indicates that the person is not someone who is well organized and to whom detail matters. In the data-processing field, such people rank low on the desirability list.

"But I'm not a writer. I know I'm a terrible speller. I'm never sure when to use a comma. I'm a lousy typist. I always have trouble with . . . ."

All of the above may be true, but each of us faces similar problems in our working lives. No one is expected to know everything or to be skilled at every task, but those who recognize their weaknesses and seek help in those areas are considered resourceful, effective, and valuable people. If you are "a lousy speller," use a dictionary or show your résumé to someone who is a good speller before putting it in its final form. Run it by friends or relatives who have experience and skills in punctuation, sentence construction, or layout and design. Most of all, be prepared to go through numerous drafts of your résumé before being satisfied with the one you'll be submitting as your best foot forward. As top writers and editors say, "All good writing is rewriting." If your résumé and, by extension, you are not worth more than one fast draft through the typewriter, that's exactly the way you're likely to be viewed by a prospective employer—not worth the time to bother interviewing.

Once you are committed to the concept of turning out a perfect résumé and have done some hard thinking about your past experiences and the accomplishments they represent, you are ready to begin the first draft. Remember, that's what it is, only a first draft, one of many, and it's part of the overall job of getting a job. This is no time to get lazy.

Here are some basic thoughts and rules about résumé writing.

• Keep it as short and simple as possible, hopefully no longer than two pages, perhaps two and a half pages (less if you have little experience). Many people have a tendency to pad their résumés with lots of extraneous and irrelevant information in order to stretch it out. Don't! The best approach is to follow the writer's adage, "If I had more time, I would have written less." It's always easier to write longer, and takes work to whittle down words so that they say the same thing in less space.

• While many professionals in the hiring business profess hard-and-fast rules about résumé length, I prefer to judge it on the basis of *readability*. If getting your résumé down to one page means cramming it onto a single sheet, leaving little room for margins and space between paragraphs, the person receiving it is going to have a difficult time reading it. In this case, it would be much better to spread the material over two pages that are pleasantly laid out and that provide a high "readability factor."

On the other hand, leaving so much white space that the résumé runs on for page after page defeats the purpose of creating a readable presentation.

Let your eye be the final arbiter (or the eye of a friend or family member who has a good sense of layout).

• One way to shorten a résumé is to take out practically all the "I's." It's assumed that the résumé you send is about you, and there is no need to stress that point by starting sentences with "I." Another way is to get rid of many of the "that" words. You'll find it will shorten and improve your writing.

• Even if padding your résumé isn't the motivation for including extraneous material, avoid the temptation. I've had countless résumés cross my desk in which the writer included so much personal information—hobbies, love of family, uninteresting and unnecessary background—that the most salient material relating to job experience was lost in the barrage of words.

• Avoid the temptation to include a "Job Objective" in your résumé, unless you're applying for a specific job with a specific company. Including a job objective on the résumé can be counterproductive. If you make it broad and vague, you accomplish nothing. If you make it extremely narrow, you cut off all possibility of being hired at that company in a similar job that does not precisely meet your stated objective.

Here's where multiple résumés are advised, however, and I would urge anyone whose background might qualify them for various positions within data processing to take this approach. Ideally, you would prepare more than one version of your résumé, each having specific applicability to a job. It doesn't mean that the bulk of the résumé changes, only that it is rearranged so that emphasis is placed on those aspects of your experience that relate directly to a given job. Let's say, for example, that you're interested in and qualified for scientific programming, commercial programming, microprocessor programming, and systems programming. My advice would be to prepare four different versions of your basic résumé, each highlighting aspects of your background that relate to those four areas of employment and, of course, each telling the truth. This takes more work, but it accomplishes a great deal. Not only does it give a prospective employer a record of your experience and training that immediately has direct applicability, but also gives the sense that you care

enough to have done a careful analysis of your qualifications and are not simply sending out an all-purpose
résumé, hoping someone will spot your qualifications
within it. Usually, preparing different versions of a
basic résumé involves little more than shifting emphasis. If it's a systems-programming job you are going
after, you will expand the job in your background that
dealt with specifics of that subspecialty, and will find
the space to do this by shortening the description of the
job you held in microprocessor programming. The
reverse will be true on that version of the résumé you
will send to employers looking for microprocessor
programmers.

• Do not include a photograph of yourself, your
salary requirements and history, or names of references. If you feel it necessary to discuss salary prior to
an interview, you can do it most effectively in a cover
letter. It does not belong on the résumé. Naming
references doesn't accomplish very much, because
employers know that you'll put down the names only
of those people who'll say nice things about you.
Besides, no one is interested in checking references
unless you have gone through the initial interview
process and are closer to being offered a job. As for
photographs, they'll see what you look like if they
decide to call you in for an interview.

So long as I'm discussing "don'ts," leave off your
résumé any mention of your race, religion, or color.
Omit names of organizations to which you belong that
may assign a race, religion, or color to you. Let the

résumé be judged on its merit. Let your résumé be devoid of anything that gets in the way.

Another no-no is being *too* candid about negative aspects of your background. There is no perfect candidate for a job. Employers understand this and assume that there are negatives in each person's background. Think of your résumé as an ad for you that presents you in the best possible light. Never lie but, by the same token, don't destroy your chances by highlighting the reasons you shouldn't be hired. Some people who have been fired will go on for a page or more explaining the reasons for the dismissal. Don't bother; no one will read it anyway, and it simply highlights the fact that you have been fired. (By the way, just about everyone has been fired from a job at some time, from a fast-food operation during high school to losing a vice-presidency at a major corporation. There's nothing to be ashamed of, so long as it doesn't represent a pattern and didn't result from illegal or unethical actions on your part.)

Don't attempt to be witty or cute in a résumé. It is not an exercise in creative writing. Rather, it is where short, factual, and gramatically correct sentences, utilizing just the right words to say what you mean, are called for.

• Stick to the basics. Use standard-size paper (8½ x 11), avoid colors other than white or off-white, and follow a basic format (which I'll discuss in a moment). Avoid the temptation to make it look like a telegram announcing your availability, or a news release heralding your emergence onto the employment scene. *Simple and basic.* If you can't sell yourself through a straightforward presentation of your business life, fancy colors and oversize paper won't help—and could hurt.

• Once you are satisfied with the contents of your résumé (and that means after numerous readings and revisions, and passing it by others who can look at it from a more detached point of view), carefully proof that version, too, and have someone else proof it before you invest in having it duplicated.

• About duplicating: after all the work you have put into your résumé, it would be a shame to make inferior copies. Avoid library or bank copying machines. Go to a printer and have it reproduced professionally. Be fair—don't use your company's photocopying or offset equipment. Besides contributing to what has become an incredible waste in American business (a survey of mine shows that 130 billion photocopies each year are unnecessary, and that 8 percent of them are for personal use), I know of several incidents where a jam occurred in the office copying machine, the service door was locked, and a page from an employee's résumé was later recovered by the boss

There's no need to have your résumé typeset. In fact, résumés printed in this manner often make a person appear to be a professional job-seeker. For that same reason, I do not generally recommend going to a résumé-preparation service. If you feel that you cannot do an effective job, write it yourself anyway and consider using a recommended service to brush up some of the wording. By actually writing your own résumé, you come to appreciate even more those aspects of your career that have value to prospective employers. Résumés that come out of these services have that cookie-cutter look, which puts you in that run-of-the-mill category. Furthermore, they are easily recognized as being professionally written, which leaves many doubts in the reader's mind as to the authenticity of the facts.

A Good, Solid Résumé Format

Obviously, your name, address, and telephone number should go at the top of the résumé. It seems too basic to even mention, but my offices have actually received some résumés without that information, making it impossible to contact the person.

The question of where to place personal data has always been debated among personnel professionals. The most common placement is at the beginning of the résumé, although many people choose to include it at the end. It really doesn't make a great deal of difference, so you might as well go with the trend, which seems to be at the beginning. Either place, keep it short and simple, including only, if you wish, your date of birth, your marital status and number of children, your height and weight, and an indication that your health is excellent, assuming that it is. Better than citing "Health excellent," refer to your attendance record on your previous jobs—if it was good. For example, "In the last two years I was absent only once for health reasons." The point about personal data is that it really has very little bearing on whether you'll be called in for an interview. It's your education, training, and, most important, accomplishments in the work field that count.

There is some debate as to where education should be placed on a résumé. My advice always is to judge its importance in the overall picture of you, and make your determination based upon that. If you have graduated from college—and a high percentage of DPers have not—and your education was computer-related, it is to your competitive advantage to put the education information up front on your résumé.

On the other hand, if you have been working in data processing for many years but are not college-educated in computer-related subjects, your education is less important and I would recommend that it go toward the end of the résumé.

Another thought about education: start with your most recent education and work backward, but if you have a college degree, omit your grammar school, junior high school, and high school.

Many recent college graduates preparing a résumé assume that because they do not have extensive work experience in data processing, there is nothing to put on their résumé except educational background. Not true. Obviously, if you do have experience in the field, you can leave out those part-time jobs you held during school. But if you are fresh out of school, listing part-time work experience is important. It gives the prospective employer a sense of your industriousness. Also, any work experience is valuable.

Now we come to the main thrust of a résumé— experience in the workplace that you hope will qualify you for the job, be it your first or your tenth.

I recommend the chronological approach, listing your most recent job first and moving through the rest of your employment history in reverse chronology. Your most recent job should be the one most thoroughly explained on the résumé, although, depending upon the particular position you are going after, jobs in your past might have even more importance and should be described in some detail. Again, let me stress that what you must get across are your *accomplishments*, not just dates and titles. What specifically did you contribute to your department's or company's efficiency, profitability, and overall success? You don't have to sound as if you're blowing your own horn. There are ways to show success and accomplishment without seeming egotistical. Tone is very important in a résumé, and it's something else you might get readings on from other people before committing yourself to the final version.

A surprising number of data processors seeking jobs leave out the essence of their experience—namely, the description of the type of hardware and software, as well as the intensity of that experience. Often, computer people are called in for an interview based exclusively on the fact that they have had hands-on experience with specific equipment and software that are of particular interest to the hiring company. This is so important that I've known some astute job seekers who have solicited those companies in their area that have similar software and hardware, using their experience with it as their selling edge. Why not?

Although I prefer the chronological approach to organizing a résumé, there are situations in which it might be more to your benefit to use the *functional* form, in which you group your experience by categories, not by years. A drawback to the functional approach is that it sometimes leads management to question whether you are hiding something, such as having been out of work for a long while. Perhaps the only time I would recommend using the functional approach is when you have had too many jobs, indicating instability, and wish to soften this. By using the functional approach, you avoid having to list each job with its corresponding dates of employment. Job hopping is particularly prevalent in data processing. I remember interviewing a man who had more than fifty jobs. I asked him about it. His answer was, "It doesn't indicate instability at all. I never quit a job."

"You mean you were fired from all of them?"

"Yes." He was proud of the fact that he did not voluntarily engage in job hopping over the course of his career.

I've met many people like that—professional job jumpers—who have little trouble getting jobs. They get them but can't hold them. You can learn from job jumpers if you stop to think why they get jobs so easily. The reason is simple: they have developed a technique that works for them through *years of practice* in changing employment. You too can practice, but without changing jobs too often, and I'll be writing about this further on in the book.

The end of your résumé can include such topics as professional affiliations, personal interests (keep them short and include only those that truly represent personal interests), and perhaps a closing comment that gives you a chance to editorialize a bit about your strengths. Frankly, I think that sort of material is better handled in a cover letter, but enough people do it on their résumé to have allowed it to gain a measure of acceptance.

Finally, *don't lie.* Embellishing your résumé might help get you an interview, but if you get an offer and your references are checked—and they very likely will be—any discrepancies on your résumé will put you in an extremely bad light. Some people who haven't finished college are tempted to indicate that they were awarded a degree. Avoid the temptation; state simply that you are continuing to work toward your degree, if you are, and leave it at that. Don't overinflate your importance on your previous job. If you do a thorough job of cataloging your accomplishments, there's no sense in running the risk of having your potential new employer discover that you can't be believed and trusted.

Everyone in business knows that a résumé is prepared to put the candidate's best foot forward. There is nothing wrong with highlighting your best qualities. Be factual, be careful in your choice of words, and when you have a résumé that has met all the requirements I've listed, use it with confidence and pride.

A Cover Letter

Each résumé you submit should be accompanied by a brief covering letter, written on your stationery and, like the résumé, carefully worded and typed—or neatly handwritten.

A cover letter is a good opportunity to get across a subtle or personal point that doesn't belong on a résumé. You can mention in the letter a particular experience in your life that has special application to the job being offered. You can indicate salary requirements, although I prefer to see that issue dealt with during interviews. You can use the cover letter to indicate that a mutual friend has suggested that you write, or to point out some interesting coincidence between your life and the life of the individual to whom you are writing, or of the company offering the job.

But, as with the résumé, avoid the temptation to be chatty and cute. A cover letter should be short. It should be direct and to the point. It should indicate that your résumé is attached, perhaps a reason for sending it to that particular person or company (in response to a newspaper ad or through the urging of a mutual friend), and should end with a positive request for consideration for the job and an opportunity for a personal interview. Many personnel experts recommend a closing line: "I will call you in a few days to follow up on this." I have mixed emotions about it. It certainly is an aggressive approach that probably works in a number of cases. It makes me a little uncomfortable, though. In effect, it puts the person on notice and has a certain threatening tone to it. The person knows that he or she will have to deal with you on the phone, like it or not—whether your résumé holds any interest or not.

I prefer a follow-up letter, rather than a phone call. The written word is wonderful in that it is placed in front of the recipient and has a chance of remaining there as a reminder that you exist and are interested in working for the company.

Another advantage of written communication is that you have the opportunity to say precisely what you wish, and not run the risk of being caught in a conversation that you're ill-prepared to deal with. Certainly, as things progress toward a specific job, and at least the initial interview has been concluded, the use of the telephone to keep in touch is valuable, but for simple follow-up after having sent a résumé and cover letter, I prefer a written note.

Ideally, the best follow-up letter or phone call should be to add something you failed to mention during the interview. This is the most subtle, most effective, and most intelligent way of saying "I want the job."

And one thing more: when writing a cover letter, make sure you have the recipient's name and title correct. Very often, we are not sure of either, which means picking up the phone, reaching the operator at the company, indicating that you wish to send correspondence to Mr. Blaine (or Blane, or Blayne), and asking for the correct spelling of the name and precise title. No one wants to see his or her name spelled incorrectly, or a wrong title used.

5

THE RÉSUMÉ WORKED— WHAT NOW?

The interview is an audition—it's your opportunity to be a star.

So far, so good. Your foot's in the door. Your résumé has been favorably received. The phone rings. They want you to come in for an interview. You can assume at this juncture that the factual material presented in the résumé concerning your experience and technical knowledge meets the parameters the employer has set for filling the job.

Now, you may assume, all you have to do is impress the interviewer during the interview and the job is yours.

Easier said than done, and the reason is that too many people now go into "automatic pilot." They assume that all they have to do is show up, be pleasant and courteous, answer a few questions, and pick a starting date. That belief goes hand in hand with previous attitudes I've discussed in this book about not needing to work hard at finding and landing a job. If there is any stage in the job-seeking process that demands thought and preparation in advance, it is getting ready for the interview.

First of all, it's time to do research on the company. The interview, especially the initial one, will give you one shot at impressing the interviewer, not only with who you are and how you handle yourself, but with how interested you are, as evidenced by what you know about the company and the people in it. By having some direct knowledge of the way the company works, you've got a head start in landing the job.

Go to the library and start researching as far in advance of the interview date as possible. Don't wait until the last minute; in fact, leaving *anything* until the last minute while pursuing a job is a mistake.

Make notes as you read. Try to find examples of things the company has done and plans for the future that directly relate to some aspect of your background and interests. In effect, you're beginning to write the *interview script*, which is an important part of the process.

It may seem surprising that I'm suggesting that you "write the script." You probably assume that the conduct of the interview will be determined solely by the interviewer and the company. But that won't be true if you've taken the time and trouble to write the script yourself, and to help determine the direction in which it will go. In fact, preparing for and going through a job interview has all the trappings of a theatrical production.

There is the script, the director of the play (interview), and the acting out of the script. Each of those elements are capable of being brought under *your control*, and to fail to take advantage of this is to lose the winning edge.

I can hear objections from data processors who see absolutely no reason to prepare for an interview other than to have their hardware and software credentials in order. True, pursuing a career in data processing is 180 degrees from preparing to go on the job-interview "stage." If you've spent your educational and employment days in front of a terminal or sitting in a mainframe room, you probably have the sort of technical knowledge and skills required for the data-processing job you are going after. A few years ago, that might have been sufficient to get that job.

Not any longer. Here's why.

Because so many talented young men and women have prepared themselves *technically* for a career in data processing, it's automatically expected that the level of technical knowledge and skills is high. Certain minimum requirements are set for a job, and only those people whose background reflects them will be called in for interviews. The problem is that there could be many candidates for the same job, each with technical skills comparable to yours.

The fact is that no matter how technically oriented the interviewer might be, he or she is a human being, responding to intangible factors in each person interviewed. It is your *performance* during the interview that will form the basis for a positive or negative reaction. The interviewer—according to our Burke studies—will respond not so much to your experience, qualifications, education, and data-processing knowledge as to your *personality*—how you *present* yourself during the interview.

Again, it is assumed that you have enough knowledge of the particular DP systems that will be utilized on the job. That's a given these days, and if you really want the job—be it your first or your fifth—you had better accept the need to prepare for your performance when the interview rolls around.

Let's get back to the concept of controlling the interview so that it puts you in the best possible light.

I make frequent appearances as a guest on nationwide television and radio talk shows. I'm confident of my ability to provide a good interview to the host or hostess, and approach those situations with the sort of confidence that only a great deal of experience brings about. However, I never approach an interview without rehearsing before ever arriving at the studio.

It works this way. The reason I've accepted the interview is that there are thoughts, ideas, or facts that I wish to get across in the brief period of time I'll be given. These things might be:

1. That a recent study of mine on "time theft"—the amount of time employees "steal" from their employers—has just been completed and released.
2. That we have recently received a prestigious award from our industry's leading trade association.

3. That we are opening several new offices within the next six months.
4. That I have been invited to testify before a Senate committee on an important piece of pending legislation having to do with my industry.

Obviously, if I go to the interview and do nothing but answer the questions the interviewer asks me, I'm not going to get those points across unless there has been a carefully agreed-upon script in advance, which is seldom the case. When it comes to a job interview, it is *never* the case.

The TV or radio interviewer might want to devote the entire interview to my thoughts on a recent Supreme Court decision on hiring practices, on an article I wrote long ago, or on my reaction to someone else's recently published book that only barely touches on my areas of expertise. Unless I write my own script prior to arriving for the interview . . . unless I've thought of ways to direct the interview to allow me to include the points that are important to me . . . unless I have rehearsed the script I've written, under my own direction . . . I'll simply be at the mercy of the interviewer. Now, when I say "script" I do not mean that I memorize words—that would create a terrible impression—but I do mean memorizing *thoughts* so I will get my important points across.

The first thing I do is to go over the points I wish to make during the interview until they are on the tip of my tongue. If I have to stop during the interview and try to remember what they were, I will lose my concentration and will be faced with a question I may not want to discuss.

As far in advance of the interview as possible, I'll work with a tape recorder and practice the answers I'm going to give, *no matter what the question.*

For example, the interviewer may say to me on the air, "I wonder what your reaction is to John Smith's book which has caused quite a stir in certain circles."

My answer, scripted by me before I ever reached the studio, might go like this: "You know, I really haven't had much time to read lately because we're in the process of expanding our network of offices around the country, and a new study we've just conducted on time theft was released yesterday. By the way, it was an interesting study. We discovered through it that . . ."

As experienced as I am in the interview setting, it would be folly for me to attempt to come up with those things off the top of my head in the midst of the pressure inherent in any interview situation. I might manage to slip in a few of the points I wish to make, but undoubtedly would leave the interview shaking my head and scolding myself for failing to work in the other two points that I considered important.

Extend this concept to the pressure of a job interview and the ramifications should be obvious.

Let's take my television-interview situation and apply it to what you face in going for that job interview the company has just called you about.

You want to set yourself aside from the rest of the field of candidates, which means you must have a firm grasp of those aspects of your experience, background, and personality that are destined to do this for you. What are they? Let's make a list, as I've done, and build it based upon those attributes we already know that employers in the data-processing field are looking for, especially things that don't appear on a nuts-and-bolts résumé.

1. While you thoroughly enjoy working in data processing, you get even more satisfaction out of end-user applications.
2. You did some work with a college or community theater, not because you have any long-term aspirations for a theatrical career, but because you thought it would help you become more confident in communicating with people.
3. You recognize the need to translate complex data-processing language into a more understandable form for those involved with computers who are not necessarily on a day-to-day working basis with it.
4. The job you are going after is in data communications, and you have recently been reading about the impressive growth of electronic mail and the movement toward a cashless society. This interests you, although it is not something you have dealt with directly, but you have kept abreast of it through reading trade journals.

Obviously, you have no way of knowing what questions the interviewer will ask, although each interview you experience should provide a basis for building a file of questions. Everyone should come out of an interview—successful or unsuccessful—and analyze what happened during it. Questions should be noted, particularly the tough ones that you had trouble handling, and they should become the basis of a continuing rehearsal for your next interview. It all comes back to the same thing: conducting your job search with the seriousness and organization you'd bring to your job. It isn't necessary to know precisely what will be asked of you during an interview in order to work in those points that you have decided are important to get across.

For example: "What is it about this job that interests you most?" the interviewer asks.

"Well, I was impressed reading about the new marketing areas you're involved with. I have also been reading a great deal about the coming cashless society and the use of electronic mail, and I think being directly involved with the sort of technology that's at the root of it will be very exciting and provide the challenges I'm looking for in my future."

Or the interviewer asks, "What kind of contributions do you think you can make to this company?"

"Obviously, I'd like to feel I was playing a part in the growth and success of the company. I guess I've always enjoyed seeing what computers could accomplish. I remember back in college when a friend of mine, who had a huge record collection, couldn't find certain songs that he was looking for. I set up a program for him and it really worked. I got a lot of pleasure out of that."

Or "Can you motivate people?"

Your answer: "Yes. I've always gotten along well

with people with whom I work, and I think that's one of the keys to success. I also think it's important for a data processor to take our technical knowledge and make it easy for others in society to understand. I've done some work with the local community theater, not because I want to be an actor, but because I really feel it's important to be a good communicator, and . . ."

George Waterman of our Kansas City franchise recently submitted a candidate to a large company. The field of candidates was extremely competitive; virtually everyone up for the job had an MBA as well as the right kind of experience. The interviewer asked, "Why should I choose you when I have more than ten MBAs with similar qualifications?" The candidate looked the interviewer in the eye and said, "When you hand me an assignment and I hand it back to you, it works. That is why you should hire me. I'll get the job done."

Our Kansas City candidate was hired. Whether he'd run across that question in other interviews and was prepared for it, or had anticipated the possibility of the question's being asked and had rehearsed an answer to it, is conjecture. Either way, he was prepared, and he gave a straightforward answer that the interviewer wanted to hear.

You can see from these examples that being ready ahead of time to handle the tough questions, and utilizing the technique of including points you wish to make while answering an interviewer's questions at the same time, can pay big dividends. You end up controlling the interview rather than being controlled by it.

I don't suggest that anyone go overboard with the

technique of working your own statements into the answer to an interviewer's question. You can't ignore a question and say only what you want to say, but you can, by practicing prior to the interview, prepare yourself to answer it smoothly. That's the key to it—*practice. Rehearsal.* Not taking an interview for granted, but preparing yourself to make optimum use of it.

The interview process is like a contest. It can't be anything else. The interviewer has an obligation to the company to hire smart and wants very much to find just the right person for the job. You, the interviewee, want to put your best foot forward so that you get the job offer. The interviewer has prepared (although some do a better job of it than others), and unless you take the initiative and thoroughly prep yourself, your chances of landing the job are diminished.

I referred earlier to the fact that the tenor of an interview will vary, depending upon whether the interviewer is part of the company's DP management, personnel department, or upper management. The variables depend upon the way the company is structured, as well as whether you're an experienced data processor or someone looking for an entry-level job.

For example, one of my studies asked data-processing managers to identify the person responsible in their companies for hiring data-processing personnel. The results:

• Entry-level data processors were hired by DP management 68 percent of the time. The personnel department of these firms was responsible approximately 14 percent of the time.

• When it came to hiring experienced data processors, DP management accounted for 74 percent while the personnel department made 12 percent of those decisions.

Although the study indicated that in most cases the data-processing manager does the actual hiring, do *not* discount the importance of the personnel executives, even though they do the actual hiring in approximately only one out of fourteen instances.

What's important to keep in mind is that each of these sources of interviewers—DP management or personnel management—will be looking for different things from you, which is why you should have a knowledge of the person who will be interviewing you so that you can adjust your script accordingly. DP managers will naturally focus more attention on your data-processing skills, although never forget that they are also responding to your personality and presentation. If you end up being interviewed by a top manager in the company (which is probably more likely in subsequent interviews, once the data-processing department has approved you), the emphasis will be more on your ability to function within the corporation and to relate to its people and goals. This interviewer will take a closer look at you as a well-rounded individual rather than as simply a technically proficient member of the data-processing department. The personnel department of a corporation approaches things from a different point of view. In many companies, the personnel department is depended upon to prescreen applicants for *every* job, which I sometimes think is the reverse of the way it ought to be. In this case, a department within the company informs Personnel that it needs an employee with certain qualifications to fill an opening. Personnel goes about the business of finding candidates by contacting a specialized data-processing recruiter, advertising in the newspaper, and sifting through résumés that have been received in the past. After the initial screening, those who have passed muster from the personnel department's point of view are sent on for interviews with the people for whom they will directly work. Naturally, people in the personnel department usually have little knowledge of the intricacies of such a complex field as data processing and will be the first to tell you that. They will be responding to you in a very general sense, to your overall appearance, demeanor, and background.

In each case, it pays you to tailor your script, rehearsal, and performance to fit the needs of the person interviewing you, for the same reason that having different versions of your basic résumé makes sense. You can't and shouldn't try to be all things to all people, and the more you can focus your background into a channel that directly reflects the needs of the person judging you, the better your chances of succeeding.

Look Your Best

Your appearance plays a more important role than you may realize. I stress this with data processors because input from specialists in Robert Half offices leaves little doubt that dress and and appearance rank low on the priority list of many DPers looking to advance in the field. Although independent studies I've commissioned indicate that appearance is not especially important in the minds of data-processing managers who do the hiring, I tend to question those findings, if only because none of us wants to admit we sometimes *do* judge a book by its cover. "It's what's inside that counts" usually sums up our public posture on the subject. The fact is, we all respond to the way a person presents himself or herself to us, particularly when we're making a decision about having that person work with us on a daily basis.

I think the major difference lies in the criterion by which we judge appearance. It has nothing to do with expensive clothing. It does have to do with clothing kept neat and clean, because that reflects upon what people think of themselves. If we don't consider ourselves worthy of shining our shoes and, by extension, don't consider the interview we're about to undergo important enough to put a shine on whatever shoes we're wearing, it says just that—this isn't important, nor am I. By the same token, sporting a beard is not unusual in our society, but not bothering to keep it trimmed, along with our hair, makes a subtle point about how we perceive ourselves and the world in which we function. Personal cleanliness and neatness, or lack of them, send out a symbolic message.

There's another reason for looking your best when going on an interview, and that has to do with the psychological impact it has upon *you*. If you're uncomfortable with the way you look, it will directly and adversely influence the way you conduct yourself during the interview. Candidates who arrive at an interview with spots on their tie or blouse are distracted by them. Instead of concentrating on the questions being asked and the answers to be given, these people keep shifting in the chair to make the spots less obvious.

The whole question of how to dress for an interview can be summed up in a couple of rules:

It doesn't matter if all the people in the data-processing department, to whom you're applying for a job, come to work in jeans and open shirts, or in slacks and sweaters. For you, not yet a member of that department, the appropriate thing is to wear business attire—a suit or dress, neatly pressed, clean, and properly fitted. Once you are hired, you will adapt your dress to fit in with those around you (only a little better), but for that first impression, it's safer to slightly overdress. You can never go wrong by being slightly overdressed at a party at which everyone else is dressed casually, but you will certainly stand out if you arrive at a black-tie affair wearing jeans.

The same principle holds true in the way you address the person interviewing you. There is absolutely no way to go wrong if you address that person as "Mr. Jones" or "Ms. Smith," unless directed otherwise. I remember a meeting I had with a senator, who was also a presidential prospect, in his office in Washington, D.C. He sat with his feet up on his desk, jacket off and tie pulled down. Some people would have taken that as an invitation to do the same. Not me. Adopting too casual an approach in the hope that it will turn the interview situation into a relaxed one almost always backfires, and this applies whether you are a veteran data processor or a recent college graduate looking to get started. Apply the basic rules of etiquette and demeanor no matter what the circumstances and atmosphere of the interviewer's office.

Handling Yourself at the Interview

Assuming that you have prepared yourself properly by learning all you can about the company, and by practicing working in the points you wish to make during the interview—and, of course, looking your best—it's now time to put everything into practice. Common sense plays a major role from this point forward, but the tension of a job interview sometimes causes us to lose some of it.

The following is a checklist of do's and don'ts that not only make good common sense but have stood the test of time.

Don'ts

• Don't be late. My surveys show that job candidates who are late for an interview will probably hurt their chances of being hired 70 percent of the time.

There's another good reason for being on time, and that is your psychological mood once the interview starts. People who run in at the last minute tend to present a frazzled, anxious front that turns off an interviewer. I always suggest to people that they show up a half hour before the interview, at least arriving in the general vicinity that early. Better to have to kill a little time with a cup of coffee than to be going through the panic of wondering whether you're going to find the right building by the appointed time.

If, for some unforeseen reason, you see that you are going to be late for the interview, find a phone booth and call. If you are really running late, it's better to cancel the interview and ask for another one rather than to arrive way beyond the time of the appointment.

• Don't chew gum or smoke. Even if the interviewer lights up, it's preferable for you not to. Recent studies of mine show that the antismoking forces are seeing their impact felt in the workplace. If the interviewer smokes, it's okay for him or her to accidentally drop ashes on the rug or to have to squint through smoke. Having the same thing happen to you will not enhance your image, even to a smoker.

If you're nervous, decline the offer of coffee and a Danish pastry. The interview is no time to fumble or to demonstrate a slight tremor in your hands. Avoid anything that might be awkward.

• Don't drink. If you are involved in an interview that takes place in a social setting, such as lunch or dinner, avoid alcohol, even if the person who is interviewing you has a drink or two. Going through a job interview is a job in itself, and drinking, even moderate drinking, dulls your senses. You can always answer with "No thank you, not right now," which indicates that you are not averse to having a drink but choose not to at the moment.

• Don't bring someone else with you to the interview. It's unprofessional to bring a friend or family member. If someone does accompany you, have them wait outside the company's building.

• Don't tell jokes. You can never be sure that the joke you tell, as mild as it might be, won't offend the interviewer. Besides, a job interview is no place for joke telling, although demonstrating a sense of humor will be in your favor. But remember, there's a big difference between telling jokes and having a sense of humor. A sense of humor means responding easily to a humorous comment or situation. Leave the jokes to professional comedians.

• Don't drag everything you own with you to the interview. If you went shopping earlier, ask the receptionist if you can leave your things in the reception room. The same with your overcoat or raincoat. You don't want to be fumbling when it's time to shake hands. Carry only your briefcase or purse into the interview with you, and keep handy materials that bear upon the interview. Always carry some extra résumés in case the one that prompted the interview has been misplaced.

• Don't use technical jargon. This is especially important for data processors because so much of DPers' daily vocabulary involves technical terms. Here is the time to make a solid evaluation of the person interviewing you. If it's someone directly connected with the company's data-processing department, you can certainly use more technical language. If, on the other hand, the interviewer is someone from the personnel department or from upper management who is not directly associated with data processing, avoid the temptation to show off your technical knowledge by spewing a barrage of computerese at that person. Rather than making a good impression, it will turn the interviewer off and make the point that you would not be the sort of employee who can evaluate the person with whom you are communicating and adjust your language accordingly.

To make the above point even stronger, let me cite the results of one of our commissioned studies that asked whether data processors are too language- and machine-oriented. Seventy-one percent of DP and top management agreed that data processors have tunnel vision concerning things other than hardware and software.

• Don't confuse ego with confidence. Every company likes to hire confident men and women, but egotistical bores are another matter. A good rule is to use the word "we" instead of "I." Instead of saying "I turned that data center into a winner," try "We all worked very hard to improve the data center and make it an efficient operation, and I think I played a significant role in it." Stress the positive about yourself, but avoid ego trips.

• Don't get into an argument. The old adage about avoiding conversations about politics and religion applies during job interviews. The same goes for any other subject that involves opinions that might set you at odds with the interviewer. Even if the interviewer has made a statement about, let's say, an opera that you, an inveterate opera buff, know is wrong, let it go. Otherwise, you may win your point, but lose the job.

Do's

• Practice proper etiquette. If you're not sure what proper etiquette is, make that part of your homework before going to the interview. There are lots of books in the library that will clue you in to what's expected. Be friendly and polite to the receptionist or secretary, who could play a role in the ultimate hiring decision. A comment like "There's a very nice young woman waiting to see you about the programming analyst job" can be a big help in preparing the interviewer to like you. Conversely, I've had a receptionist tell me that an obnoxious person was waiting to be interviewed. That candidate's chances of getting the job added up to zero before the interview ever began.

Like a photograph, a smile is worth ten thousand words, so don't be reluctant to display a friendly, sincere smile to everyone you meet. Shake hands firmly but avoid being a "cruncher." Look people in the eye, but don't overdo it. When you are asked a question, it's a perfect time to move your focus of attention from the interviewer and to take a couple of seconds to think about the answer. Thoughtful people are viewed more positively that those who have a flippant answer.

• Be observant. Whenever I make a speech, I always look for things in the lobby of the auditorium or at the dais that I can work into my opening remarks. It gives those people listening to me a sense that I care about them and am not simply delivering a canned speech.

The same holds true when going for a job interview. There may be things in the office that represent a common interest with the interviewer. If the pictures of the interviewer's children indicate that they are the same age as your children, it's worth commenting on. Books on the desk, framed awards on the wall, and the way in which the office has been decorated are all potential sources of opening comments by you that can set a more relaxed tone and establish a bond between you. As with everything else, however, don't overdo it; don't reach. Better to say nothing than to come off as a phony.

• Be enthusiastic. Hiring surveys we've conducted over the years indicate that as many as 90 percent of interviewers rate enthusiasm as an extremely important qualification for being hired. Be pleasant, warm, courteous, and responsive, and radiate energy and interest.

• Make sure the conversation is two-way. Don't interrupt a talkative interviewer, but find ways to get your points across in the limited time you have. And be a good listener. When DP management and top management were asked in one of our studies whether data processors are poor listeners, 45 percent of those who answered the question said DPers *are* poor listeners. If you are a success-oriented data-processing profession-al, sharpen up those listening skills.

• Ask for the job if you have come to the conclusion that you really want it and that your changes of being hired are pretty good. By asking for the job, I don't mean pleading for it. Prove that you want it by showing confidence in yourself and in your ability and willing-ness to do everything necessary to make the employer happy that he or she hired you. You might say, "Ms. Jones, I like the company, I like the job, and I would like working for you—and if I'm hired, I can assure you that I won't let you down."

• Volunteer. If there is a lingering question about some aspect of your experience or background, con-sider offering to do something without compensation in order to prove yourself. I don't recommend this for all jobs for which you are interviewed, but if one really appeals to you, don't be afraid to demonstrate the kind of interest and aggressiveness that companies like to see.

• End on an up beat. Come away from every inter-view with something positive. If you are told by the interviewer that you just don't measure up in terms of qualifications, don't fail to ask the interviewer to rec-ommend other executives in the field who might have openings that more appropriately fit your credentials. If the interview concludes with you feeling confident about your chances, state your enthusiasm and ask what the next step might be.

• Take some time to review as soon as possible after you've left the interview. There undoubtedly will have been questions that you could have answered more smoothly, and you should practice your responses to those questions before going to the next interview. Chances are they will come up again. Many interview questions have become standardized.

• Keep practicing. If you have gone through several interviews without landing a job, don't be discouraged and start tucking your head under your wing. Use the interview process to build your network of contacts, and recognize that being turned down for a job does not indicate a lack of worth on your part. Competition may have been very keen for the opening.

• Be organized. If you have kept good records of the jobs you've applied for and the interviews you've experienced, you will have a solid sense of the timetable of those events. Sometimes a company will hire someone and, after a month or so, realize that they made the wrong choice, or the person hired will leave because another job opening that had been unresolved has come through. For those companies and jobs that you keenly wanted, by all means drop a note to the person who interviewed you, or telephone, and show your continued interest in the company. They might be so impressed with that approach that they find another slot within the organization for you.

A good actor or actress constantly goes over each performance in a search for ways to improve. Athletes scrutinize videotapes of their actions in order to discover small flaws that are getting in the way of their success.

A job seeker is no different, especially where the interview is involved.

6

NOW THAT YOU'VE LANDED A NEW JOB

Getting off on the right foot will prevent you from being left behind.

If you have viewed your search for a new job in data processing as a *job*, and have utilized the ideas and techniques in previous chapters, you've probably received job offers (and I'm confident in using the plural because of the great demand for good people in DP). Hopefully, you are deciding between jobs, or have made your choice and are about to start a new one.

If you are debating whether to accept a certain job, here are a few things to keep in mind:

• Are the offers firm? The scenario is an old one and, unfortunately, repeats itself with regularity. So many people—particularly if they have been looking for a while—read more into an employer's words than is intended. For instance, after going through a few interviews you're told, "You're the person we're really interested in. It looks good for you."

That's *not* a firm offer, but people take it as such and drop out of the job-search market. Some even quit their current job and go on vacation, only to return to be told that someone else has come along with better qualifications and has been hired.

A firm offer means a direct and specific commitment, including a starting date, definite salary agreement, and dealing with the personnel department about the details of hiring.

• Assuming that your offer is firm, the next question is whether you really *want* the job. It should be assumed that you have given this a lot of thought throughout your initial exposure to the company. Hopefully, the research you did on the firm before being interviewed gave you good insight into its reputation, future expectations, and general industry and community standing. If you have any doubts about it, call the person who will be your boss and ask for another conversation about the job. Use that opportunity to do a little more sizing up of the place and its people. Do those you come in contact with seem happy? Are they pleasant, or does their mood represent a general dissatisfaction with the company and with their job?

A young woman I know, who had been offered a position as a programmer at a medium-size manufacturing company, took the trouble to go through back issues of the local newspaper. It seems that this company was besieged with union problems. Walkouts and job actions were almost a monthly occurrence. That bothered her, and before committing herself to the firm she aggressively pursued another job that had seemed promising but hadn't come through as yet. Her aggressiveness paid off. She got the second job and politely turned down the first.

• It's been said that a lot of weddings take place because the bride and groom are too embarrassed to cancel at the last minute, even though one or both of them sense deep down that they are making a mistake. I suspect that a number of people take jobs for the same reason.

Don't be reluctant to politely decline a job offer for fear of hurting someone's feelings. The company won't hesitate for a moment to turn *you* down, and you should have the same attitude.

• Another evaluation that you should make (and that should be on your mind throughout your exposure to the company) is whether this job meets your long-term career goals in data processing. Working in a mediocre department, with equipment and software that are not current and in demand, can hinder your career rather than enhance it. The job itself may appear to be attractive, and the salary might be right at this stage in your career, but if it is the sort of dead-end position that many DPers ultimately find themselves in, rethink the offer. Of course, no job need be a dead end for individuals who use their imagination to broaden their particular job's scope, or who use it as a means of developing skills, experience, and contacts to help them move on to other positions within the firm, or with other companies. However, specific situations can make those things more difficult to accomplish. For instance, is the company in a period of growth, or are its fortunes on a downward trend? The industry itself might be "soft," or the company's financial position shaky. It's difficult to look for advancement and monetary rewards in a company that is in the process of pulling in the strings in order to survive. Of course, landing the right job in a company that is beginning to turn around can be an open door to great future success for individuals who are there at the right time to contribute to the turnaround.

• What about the executive to whom you'll be reporting? Is he or she in a secure, powerful position within the firm? That's important, because if a supervisor's position is weak, everyone under him or her deals from a weakened posture. It's hard to ascertain this without actually working with that person for a period of time, but it's worth a little exploration, perhaps with friends who have worked at that company or with a competitor. You don't want to appear to be snooping, but you can say, "I've been offered a wonderful job at XYZ Corporation, working for John Jones. He seems like a nice guy. Do you know anything about him?"

I assume that money and benefits have been discussed and are to your liking. If they are—and everything else about the job seems to end up on your positive list—you'll enthusiastically accept it. I can't imagine why you wouldn't.

How to Say Good-bye

If you are coming into your new job in data processing from having been unemployed, or straight out of college, you are not faced with the need to resign from your present employment.

For some reason, countless men and women view resigning as the simplest of acts: tell your boss you have found another data-processing job for more money, or with more challenge, and leave it at that.

That isn't sufficient, not if you are setting your sights on a long-term and successful career in the field.

I write a monthly column in *Management Accounting Magazine* called "Managing Your Career." A young man wrote and asked my advice on the proper way to resign from his present job. My basic response was to congratulate him for caring enough about the resignation process to seek advice in the first place. That attitude will stand him in good stead over the course of his working life.

The key ingredient in resigning is to leave on the most positive of terms. It isn't a time to vent your frustrations with the job, company, or boss, nor is it a time to tell your immediate supervisor what's wrong with the way the data-processing department is run. If you have established a friendly relationship with your boss and are asked for your evaluations prior to leaving, that's one thing, but avoid falling into the trap of gratuitously offering negatives.

Your resignation should be in person, followed by a short, courteous letter confirming your intention to leave, stating the date of your departure, and, I recommend, adding a line of two indicating how much you have enjoyed your time with the company, how much it has contributed to your knowledge and growth, and how you hope to keep in touch with its people in the ensuing years.

The reason a verbal resignation is not sufficient is that it puts nothing in your file. A few years from now—should you be looking for a reference from that firm—that letter of resignation, when dragged out of the file by someone who never knew you, establishes a positive view of you in that stranger's mind.

Some final thoughts on resigning:

• Don't succumb to the temptation to confide in your boss that you are "thinking of leaving." This compromises your employer's position as a manager and can set up bad feeling when you actually do resign.

• Keep it professional. If you have a good working relationship with your current boss, be prepared for the possibility that he or she might take your resignation as a personal rejection. With these people especially, it's important to keep the reason for leaving on a purely career basis, stressing that the new job offers certain challenges within data processing that you feel you should pursue.

If possible, give one month's notice, and use your remaining weeks on the job to enhance your reputation with the firm you are leaving. Go all out with a replacement brought in for you before you depart. The last few weeks on a job is not the time to relax and do less work. Take the opposite view and give it 100 percent.

Resist bragging about the new job to your fellow employees. That will only create bad feeling. And don't breach any confidences built up during your years with the firm. Make an extra effort to establish close bonds with your fellow employees. Networking, at all levels of a career, is one of the most effective ways to build it over the long haul, and establishing and keeping contacts will always benefit you.

Early Going in the New Job

Starting a new job is always exciting, as well as anxiety-provoking. The reasons for it—aside from the natural emotions connected with going into *anything* new—will vary depending upon whether you are coming to the job from a period of unemployment or right out of college, or have been climbing the data-processing ladder and are taking your next step.

Coming out of college to a first job involves problems that primarily have to do with making a shift from the academic world to the reality of nine-to-five (DPers will laugh at my use of those hours to indicate a normal workday in the field).

For someone coming out of a long period of unemployment, having a job to go to will be a relief, a welcome haven from the confusing and discouraging days of not working.

People changing jobs within data processing bring

with them two valuable assets to make the transition easier: hands-on experience with the tools of the trade and prior exposure to the functioning of the business world, at least within the confines of a data-processing department.

But while the hardware and software might be identical to those in your previous job, you can count on significant differences in the way your new department and company are run. There are many factors at play here, and one of the most important is what is termed "corporate culture."

Every family has differences within it that set it apart from its neighbors, and the same holds true for companies, large and small, service and manufacturing, established and start-up alike. Understanding the corporate culture that surrounds your new job will play a large role in how well you succeed in it, and will help determine your future success.

Keys to Your New Company's Culture

It's tricky for someone new on a job (I define "new" to mean the first six months) to get a firm grip on what the company's culture truly is. The reason for this is that many companies espouse one culture while living another, and the espoused culture is often the one that a new employee embraces.

For example, a smaller company in the business of developing new and innovative software might have been founded and headed by young, aggressive executives whose daily business and personal actions smack of impetuousness and a penchant for risk-taking. That would be the image that you would be most likely to perceive as representing the entire company, and you might find that you pattern yourself after those top people. The problem arises when, further down the management line, your immediate supervisor functions more methodically and without the capacity or willingness to go out on a limb. That puts you in a dilemma: your immediate supervisor responds favorably to a slower-moving, cautious individual and does not take kindly to a more flamboyant style, even though it represents top management.

The same conflicts can occur in virtually every area of a company. The top executives might be extremely informal, while middle management takes a more formal approach to relations between management and employees.

The nature of the industry in which the company functions will determine, to a great extent, that company's culture. An aircraft manufacturer, whose future rides on an extremely long-term and sizable commitment to one product with the hope that it will be widely accepted over the years, places greater value on employees whose approach to decision making is less crisis-oriented. Data processors who can view the job in terms of a marathon runner, rather than a sprinter, will be more comfortable in such a culture.

On the other hand, a company engaged in the manufacture of a product that must constantly be refined to meet the competitive demands of the marketplace will place a premium on people who are able to rapidly shift gears and respond to immediate change.

If you have been in data processing for a while and have taken the time—and used the experience—to understand yourself and the way you function best, you will naturally gravitate toward a company with a corporate culture that approximates your style. In terms of career growth, it is very important that you do this on a continuing basis, and use the knowledge as a guide for future decisions.

Adapting to a corporate culture is difficult for everyone, but it's likely to be more difficult for data processors. The field of data processing has its own *occupational culture,* and very often it doesn't match up with a given *corporate culture.* From the very beginning, data processing has attracted men and women who held themselves outside the mainstream of American business life and who functioned with the philosophy that all they needed for future success was to make a computer stand on its ear and perform. Those days are over, and it is the blending of the DPers' culture with the American business culture that is necessary for the continued success of both.

That's not to say that data processors must lose their identity. Rather, it is like the varied ethnic cultures that have made this country great. An ethnic group will continue to enjoy its unique characteristics within itself, but also spreads out into the broader American culture and uses the process of assimilation to contribute to that larger culture.

The same holds true in business.

Culture + Politics = Blend

One of the major problems in blending cultures—occupational, corporate, or ethnic—is our reluctance to shed the myth-belief system by which we live our lives.

It works this way. We are brought up with a set of myths given us by our family, friends, schools, and surrounding society. I'm not using the term "myth" in a negative sense, only to make the point that a great deal of what we end up believing in our adult lives is not necessarily based upon reality. It's more *mythical*: for example, "Just do your job and you'll be rewarded" or "Security is found only in a large corporation" or, "Politics is a dirty word and shouldn't be engaged in by anyone except politicians."

The myths with which we grow up are legion, and many of them eventually harden into our *belief system*. The myth, as unfactual as it might be, now is practiced as though it is based on rock-hard data. The word "myth" is a good example. We tend to view it as something totally lacking in substance, a fairy tale, yet the word does not have to be perceived that way.

The same holds true for the word "politics." There is, of course, dirty politics; one needs only to read the daily newspaper to be given examples of that. But if the word "politics" is used in the true sense of its definition (the ability to persuade people to our way of thinking), its function in the business world takes on a greater and more valuable meaning.

Politics plays a pervasive role in every company, and employees who refuse to at least acknowledge that, and who live their professional lives acting upon the *myth* that it is something to be avoided (because it has become a *belief*), will not only find it virtually impossible to blend their occupational culture with that of the company, but will soon find their career growth stymied, not only within that company but within the data-processing field itself.

One myth about office politics is that it involves stabbing people in the back in order to get ahead. People who do that are not practicing politics; they're simply bad people. Assigning the word "politics" to them gives it an unnecessarily bad name.

Politics in the workplace involves an understanding of the relationship of people within a department and the relationship of that department to the company as a whole, and, ultimately, how that company will relate to the industry within which it functions.

For men and women beginning a career in data processing, politics often doesn't seem important, but as a person grows in a career (assuming you're someone who wishes to grow and not simply stagnate at one level), understanding and becoming an effective user of politics is a necessity.

For example, let's say you have been doing a good job in programming and programming analysis, a typical steppingstone level in data processing. Your intermediate goals are to move up to positions in systems analysis and project leadership, with your eyes set on the eventual position of manager of information services. If those are your aspirations, being comfortable with the use of politics as earlier defined not only can't be avoided, but must play a continuous role in your thinking.

At lower levels of data processing, technical knowledge looms larger than it does as you proceed up through the various layers of responsibility. For instance, DP managers have to be concerned not only with the technical operations of their department, but with how their department contributes to the company's overall goals. A typical situation would be when the managers of a large and important warehouse needs a workable data system to keep track of inventory. At the same time, a skilled analyst working under the manager has no interest in something so mundane as keeping track of spare parts, and would much rather be working on the development of a more esoteric system. The manager must come up with a way to satisfy the needs of the warehouse and at the same time keep his or her best analyst motivated. How do managers do that? They practice *politics*, in its purest form.

Getting Along

It's harder to fire, lay off, or demote a pleasant person than an unpleasant one.

Pleasant people don't have to stop to think about how they present themselves to their fellow employees on a daily basis. People who *aren't* naturally pleasant should stop and ponder this, from a business point of view.

Just as personality plays a large role in the hiring

process, it continues to influence each person's career advancement. It seems so simple, yet many people fail to realize it and eventually find themselves falling behind and wondering why.

Because data processing tends to be an insular occupation (less so today), the people working in it tend to lose sight of the fact that there is a broader world outside the DP department that is made up of *people*, and that getting along with them is a necessity if that broader world is to be explored and conquered. It comes down once again to the reality that technical competence, while important in the beginning stages of a data-processing career, becomes less so as a person advances.

The reason an interviewer will choose someone with a bright, pleasant, and warm personality is axiomatic: when you have a pool of people from which to hire, and the people in that pool are equally competent, you might as well bring into the organization someone who will be a pleasure to spend each day with.

The same holds true when considering people for promotion. No one wants to deliberately bring into their sphere a sourpuss or someone lacking in a sense of humor, which so often can make the difference between a tense, strained data-processing department and one that functions smoothly under pressure.

Speaking of a sense of humor, a survey I did of top executives in corporations across America showed that a sense of humor is, indeed, an important ingredient in business success. The survey—which asked personnel directors and vice-presidents of a hundred of America's top one thousand corporations whether people with a sense of humor were better, the same as, or worse at their jobs than people with little or no sense of humor—indicated that 84 percent felt that employees who had a good sense of humor did a better job than their dour colleagues. Why? Because people with a sense of humor tend to be more creative, less rigid, and more willing to consider and embrace new ideas and methods, to say nothing of being a pleasure to be with.

Getting along with people can be considered a *political act*—or art; another reason that the term "politics" should not be viewed in a negative light. None of this suggests being a phony, but it does stem from my belief that as long as anyone is going to bother getting up in the morning and going to work, they might as well be pleasant about it. It enriches the working lives of those around them and, ultimately, can help enrich their own professional lives.

The same principle can be applied to the way you dress on the job. Whatever the prevailing dress code of your department and company, taking the trouble to wear clean and pressed clothing that portrays an upbeat, caring personality and being well groomed make a positive statement about you. We all like to be around men and women like this and prefer to avoid those who don't care about how they look.

If your eye is set on becoming part of upper management, consider that when choosing the clothes you wear to work each day. The DP department might be casual, but it usually isn't that way in the executive suite.

Joan Bernstein, our data-processing specialist in the Robert Half New York office, comments, "Management expects DPers to be 'regular people,' as well as fitting the corporate image. From what I have observed, DP and Brooks Brothers make a likely team for the eighties."

Get Off to a Fast Start

A friend of mine who was an Air Force officer during the Korean conflict once told me that the saddest day in his military life was when he was promoted from second lieutenant to first lieutenant. The promotion was automatic; the first eighteen months of his life as a young officer were spent wearing the gold bars of a second lieutenant. Then, after that year and a half, came the promotion to first lieutenant, which carried with it silver bars on his shoulders. "As long as I was wearing those gold bars," he said, "everyone was tolerant of my mistakes. Those bars told everyone that I was new. Then, once the silver went on my shoulders, I didn't have any more excuses for fouling up. It was traumatic."

Every new employee is given a grace period, its length depending upon that person's experience in the workplace. It's generally accepted that newcomers will be given more time to acclimate and to get into the job than more veteran men and women, who are expected to apply their previous knowledge and experience a lot faster.

In either case, it behooves you to get started contributing to the department and company as quickly as possible. Employers like new employees who fall into the category of "self-starter," an overused but significant description of a person who doesn't wait to be led by the hand but who takes initiative and seeks out projects.

Data-processing specialists in my organization urge all people they've placed to get going on the job as quickly as possible, once they have had a few days to settle in. Ed Lance, the data-processing placement manager in our Milwaukee franchise, puts it this way: "Try to do something significant within the first thirty days."

What constitutes a significant contribution within the first month of employment? Lance lists these three items:

1. Fix a long-standing problem.
2. Install a new package.
3. Modify an existing program and put it into production.

This doesn't mean that you should forge ahead like a bull in a china shop and start delving into programs about which you have little knowledge. It doesn't mean that you should take on a project without permission from your supervisor. It *does* mean, however, that by looking for projects with which to begin contributing to the data-processing department, you indicate to management that you have as much of a business sense as you do a data-processing sense. The project doesn't have to be large—in fact, it should be small enough to allow you to complete it within a reasonable period of time—but it should be something that eliminates a headache that someone in the department has mentioned, or that improves on an existing program in terms of the time expended or the cost to the company.

The best way to get into the flow of your new job and department is to be a good listener and to ask questions. People tend to resent a newcomer's immediately offering opinions about how the department is run, but most people respond favorably to those who have just arrived and who demonstrate sufficient interest to be asking about the way things are done.

Pick your time for asking questions, however. Don't interrupt a meeting or bother someone deeply involved in a project. Look for those moments when there is a lull, or perhaps a social moment with someone you have befriended who can give you an indication of areas in which you might be of immediate help.

Volunteer for Everything

The old army adage says, "Volunteer for nothing." In business, the opposite is true, particularly for someone coming in new to an organization. Starting a new job is the perfect time to expend extra energy. It might mean longer hours, at least initially, but that kind of initiative can establish a foundation for you within the company, one that will have a lingering positive effect.

Every department has necessary jobs that people

tend to shun. Those are exactly the jobs that you should make yourself available for. It doesn't mean becoming a patsy. Rather, it says that not only are you a hard worker and willing to get your hands dirty, but you recognize your *newness* to the organization and are willing to work your way into the hierarchy. Taking on the less-desirable jobs and *getting them done* ranks high on an employer's list of traits to be admired and rewarded.

What are attributes that every boss looks for? Here are a few:

• *Get things done.* So many people spend their working days exploring ways to accomplish a task, rather than attacking and finishing it. Learn what you need to know about a particular job and *do it!* Better to complete a job, even though it has areas needing improvement, than to continue asking questions and never get to it. A finished product can be improved; you can't improve on something you haven't started.

• *Make no excuses.* With the exception of crisis-type situations, a boss does not want to hear why a job wasn't done. Again, *do it;* don't explain it away.

• *Set realistic goals and keep your superior informed of progress.* Promising to complete a task in an impossibly short period of time and then having to report that it isn't done (with the inherent excuses) impresses no one. As for keeping your manager informed of your progress, it doesn't mean belaboring the point with repeated conversations. A periodic short note will do, and leave the excuses out of it. The assumption is that you'll complete the job in the allotted amount of time.

In line with this, don't hesitate to inform your superior of bad news having to do with a project. Again, pick your time; don't lay bad news on your boss at the end of the day, or just as he or she is going out to lunch. But be quick to let superiors know of legitimate problems that have developed that might eventually reflect unfavorably upon them and their department. Never leave your boss open to negative suprises. If you happen to work for someone who can't tolerate bad news, it might be time for you to put your feelers out for another job.

• *Suggest answers.* If you must bring a problem to your superior, carry along a few solutions. Bosses have enough of their own problems and expect those working for them to have explored answers before laying problems on the desk.

• *Be a good listener.* For instance, if your boss says to you, "I've been thinking about having you take over this project," it probably means you will be taking it over. People try to avoid giving direct orders, preferring to state ideas and then wait for everyone within earshot to act upon them. A good boss will be more direct, but that doesn't get you off the hook. Learn to listen and to interpret.

• *Get along with your co-workers.* Your boss wants results and won't take kindly to squabbles between employees being at the root of failure. In line with that, make it a point to spread your wings and meet people outside your department. One of the most valuable things you can contribute to a department is an understanding of the problems others are having that might affect the work you and your peers are doing. For instance, if you learn at lunch in the cafeteria that another division is having a particularly pressing problem that your group might be able to solve, bring that knowledge back to your superiors. That information can trigger action in your department that, if successful, will boost the esteem of your boss and your department in the eyes of upper management.

• *Develop a sense of order.* Stay late a few evenings, or come in on the weekend to organize your workplace. The first days on a job are often chaotic and confusing. If you allow that chaos to dictate how you set up your physical surroundings, you establish a potentially troublesome situation. It goes back to the concept of organizing yourself during the job-search phase of your career. It's extremely annoying for a busy executive to ask someone in the department for an important piece of paper and be told it can't be found. Being organized takes extra effort; however, it not only pays off in avoiding that kind of situation, but ultimately saves you time and effort.

• *Contribute to your own "personnel file."* I mentioned earlier the importance for everyone to establish their own set of records indicating the contributions they have made to the company in the event that it's time to ask for a raise or a promotion, or to prepare a résumé in search of another job. Don't let this slide. All it takes is a hastily scribbled note in a file folder or notebook. When the time comes to call upon it, the material is there and you won't have to depend upon vague recollections of past achievements and contributions.

• *Be a team player.* I can't stress enough the need for all persons in an organization, no matter what the job, to view their activities as part of an overall corporate objective. The company wants profits, and the activities of everyone within it should be devoted to that goal. No one stands alone in a company, and it is the interaction of employees that ultimately decides a company's success or failure. Nothing is more important for your career growth than to develop and nurture this philosophy. Team players are valued in a business; loners are not.

So much of how you choreograph your early days on a new job will depend upon your individual and unique attributes and needs. There is room in any business, no matter how structured, for your individuality to bloom. The trick is to incorporate *you* into the overall scheme of the company and to look for ways to apply what you're all about to that larger picture.

Assuming that you have happily and productively settled into your new job, what else should you be thinking about in terms of continued growth, either with that company or with others in the data-processing world?

That's next.

7
ATTITUDE FOR SUCCESS

*Success doesn't happen to those who wait
for it to happen.*

The book to this point has been devoted to getting a job in data processing. It should be evident from what you've read that seeking a job involves a set of specific and tangible rules, all calculated to make the most of your education, experience, and personality.

Now, however, we move into a less tangible area—the question of *attitude for success*. This has less to do with résumés and interview techniques, and places greater emphasis on *you*.

There is a technique that many successful people use when called upon to prepare a proposal. First, they meet with the person for whom the proposal is intended, in order to find out what elements that person considers most important. Once that's done, they include those ingredients in the proposal, which, in virtually every instance, results in enthusiastic acceptance and approval.

The same principle can be applied by each of you looking to achieve maximum career success in data processing. What are those people in positions of power looking for from DPers seeking advancement? The best way to answer that, I think, is to refer to the studies I conducted within the data-processing field.

The first study asked DP managers and top management what they considered the most important traits or attributes of a good data processor. Here were the results:

Under the heading of *personal attributes* they listed the following traits in order of importance:

Ability to be logical
Ability to interact/get along with people
Communications skills
Open-minded/receptive/willing to learn/willing to
    change
Creative/good imagination
Patient
Personality

These same people, when asked to evaluate *skills and abilities*, came up with these, again in order of importance:

Technical expertise
Problem-solving abilities
Well trained/knowledgeable about equipment/how
    to use equipment
Intellectual ability
Math skills
Management skills/project control/project planning

When it came to *working habits,* the results looked like this:

Good working habits
Hard worker
Accurate
Efficient/organized

Finally, when it came to the *background* of good data processors, the respondents to the study pinpointed:

Education
Business perspective/understand client needs
Experience

Let's couple this with the second study, which was devoted to the question of why some data processors fail to get ahead. Again, the respondents were from data-processing management as well as from top management.

Under the general heading of *lack of motivation,* these findings came to light:

Lack of motivation/drive
Lack of initiative
No ambition to get ahead
Don't work hard enough

Under *personal attributes,* the reasons given for data processors failing to get ahead were:

Inability to relate with/work with people/hard to get
    along with
Inability to communicate/express self clearly

Lack of personality
Not a good listener

Another category was *lack of understanding*. Included under this were:

Not understanding big picture/not relating tasks to
   big picture
Not understanding business administration/how
   business is run
Not understanding company's objectives

Finally, those who felt that being *underqualified* was at the root of DPers' failure to advance said:

Inexperience
Lack of technical skills/expertise
Lack of adequate education
Chose wrong career
Not qualified for job

Naturally, the importance given each of these traits differs somewhat among data-processing managers and top management, the significant differences occurring when it comes to such points as not understanding the big corporate picture or company objectives, and the inability to relate to others or to communicate clearly.

Working hard, motivation, and initiative were important to both classes of respondents.

What's to be taken from these findings is that men or women looking to advance—not only within data processing, but into those areas that involve end use—have to continually evaluate themselves and take whatever steps are necessary to round themselves out to meet the requirements of loftier jobs.

At the same time, the *attitude for success* must be present.

What is *attitude for success?*

There are probably as many ways to sum it up as there are people who have thought about it. It involves wanting to win. It means viewing accomplishment as a goal unto itself. It stems from a genuine joy in working hard and being willing to put yourself on the line. It's men and women who view the glass as being half full rather than half empty, and who are open to the world around them and view it with an intense sense of curiosity and wonder.

Authors and philosophers have tried to define it over the ages.

The philosopher Nietzsche said:

> *If ye would go up high, then use your own legs!*
> *Do not get yourselves carried aloft;*
> *Do not seat yourselves on other people's*
> *backs and heads!*

And George Bernard Shaw wrote:

> *The people who get on in this world are the*
> *people who get up and look for the circum-*
> *stances they want, and, if they can't find*
> *them, make them.*

Having the proper attitude for success is essential to being successful. You can possess all the technical skills and knowledge available, and have all the other trappings of a winner, but if you aren't looking to win and aren't willing to work hard enough to achieve a victory, you won't. It's that simple.

Here are some questions to ask yourself about your attitude for success.

Do I Like What I'm Doing?

It goes without saying that successful people enjoy what they do, and it's hard for someone working at a job they don't like to muster the enthusiasm to succeed. As Malcolm Forbes, one of America's most successful businessmen, said to me, "If you don't like what you're doing, you'll never be successful. I don't think anybody does something really well unless they truly enjoy what they do."

This goes back to the concept of knowing yourself before ever entering the field of data processing. For many, the occupation they choose to pursue is the right one from the beginning. For others, it takes exposure to the occupation before coming to the realization that a mistake has been made. If you feel you have made a mistake and would be better served in another field, by all means change. There are countless success stories of people who came to that conclusion at some point during their lives, switched into an entirely different line of work, and became wildly successful.

By the way, most people who achieve success in data processing seem to have known what they were doing when they chose to pursue DP as a career. When we asked members of data-processing management whether they would choose the field if they had it to do over, 80 percent of them agreed that they were pleased with the profession and would indeeed make the same decision. Only 10 percent disagreed, and 10 percent did not have an opinion about it. Because the respondents to this study had achieved a certain level of success in data processing, the results support the contention that liking what you do helps in achieving success.

My one caution to you—should you feel data processing is wrong for you—is that you be sure that it is the field you're unhappy with, and not yourself and the world in general. Psychiatrists recognize that there are two kinds of depression, *reactive* depression and *general* depression. We all become depressed over the death of a loved one, the loss of a job, or other factors of life that affect us. That kind of depression is healthy and normal. Then there are those who are simply depressed in general and who go through life with a negative, pessimistic view of the world. For these people, depression is not healthy and normal; they need help.

The same situation exists with people who, rather than looking inside themselves, are constantly blaming externals for their unhappiness. It could be that your dislike of data processing is so pervasive and real that a career change is definitely in order. On the other hand, make sure that you are not using your occupation as an excuse for what is basically a downbeat, negative, and pessimistic attitude.

Am I Willing to Work Hard Enough to Achieve Success?

There's hard work, and there's *hard* work. Some people refer to those who put in just enough effort to get the job done as staying within the "comfort zone." Then there are others who are willing to go out of that zone and give that extra effort. The willingness to work hard and to go beyond what is expected of us is of primary importance if success is to be achieved. We've all run across it countless times: some individuals resent people who have achieved great success and its inherent monetary rewards, but would never be willing to make the sacrifices those people had to make. We achieve success in direct proportion to the effort we are willing to expend in its pursuit. I'm not suggesting that in order to be successful we have to become workaholics. The truly successful people I know have found a way to put in long hours on the job and still have time for vacations, hobbies, and family. What they *don't* allow in their lives are periods of time in which nothing is accomplished. These are active people who work hard and play hard, and who have a sense that hard work brings the sort of riches—monetary and otherwise—that we all desire.

An example is the actor Alan Alda. He commuted between his home on the East Coast and California, where the weekly episodes of "M*A*S*H" were shot, and said during an interview that on his way home after a week of shooting, he had to gear himself up for the "job" of being a husband and father with the same intensity as when he was mentally readying himself for a week of acting. He had recognized that hard work is the key to success, personal and professional, and he obviously is the sort of individual willing to exert considerable effort in both aspects of his life.

We have to work hard at our personal lives, including relationships, and our careers demand the same if we are to find fulfillment in them. If, in analyzing your attitude for success, you realize that you are not the sort of person who gets "high" on hard work and on completing goals, you had better either begin working on it or resign yourself to not achieving much more than you currently have.

Am I Willing to Take Risks?

If you are someone who is content with small risks and small gains, significant success might be out of your reach. Actually, this attribute of the successful person—the willingness to make decisions and suffer the consequences—can be combined with a more conservative, limited set of goals. We're not talking about being reckless. What we are referring to is working within the confines of your current job and making sure it gets done right, while at the same time reaching into other areas. Successful people in every walk of life have been willing to go after something new on the horizon. Most of these people have failed at least once, but they don't view failure as defeat. Instead, they learn from it, keep looking for opportunities, and get on with their lives with the same verve and resolve as before the failure.

Am I Okay? Are You Okay?

Successful people celebrate not only their own lives, but the lives of those around them. One of the most popular psychology books ever written was titled *I'm OK, You're OK*. Put most simply, it analyzes the way we relate to the world around us. For instance, criminals generally have the attitude "I'm okay, you're not okay," referring to their victims and society at large. Then there are those people whose self-esteem is so low that they view the world from a "You're okay, I'm not okay" perspective.

Healthy people deal with the world from the standpoint of the book's title: "I'm okay, you're okay." In other words, we're all okay, you and me, and we'd better get along on this earth.

Some of us fail to realize that no matter how sophisticated the technology surrounding us is, no matter how large the industry and product it represents, no matter what the future holds in terms of robots and an electronic society, *people* are at the heart of it. A key ingredient for success is to recognize this and to develop interpersonal skills that allow us to function smoothly and happily with others.

The successful manager or executive knows how to deal with the dual objective of keeping staff happy while contributing to the company's goals. Some people are naturally better at it than others, but everyone can learn to improve. It takes the desire to do so and a willingness to be introspective enough to analyze our faults and to act upon that knowledge.

Do I Know What I'm Doing Today?

Successful people are goal-directed. They have a sense of what they're going to accomplish this day, this week, this month, and over an even longer period. That doesn't mean they are rigid about how they use their time. Far from it. In fact, they also possess the ability to shift gears quickly as the occasion demands. Although they might be detoured from time to time, they never lose sight of the overall goal they have set for themselves, even if it means adding extra hours to the day or week in order to accomplish it. Success demands a sense of purpose, and people who flounder through the day because they haven't established clear-cut priorities and goals are the ones who flounder in their careers.

Do I View Myself as a Victim?

Successful people don't trust to luck. They take responsibility for their successes and failures, and for their lives. Winners don't make excuses for failure, nor do they chalk up their successes to luck. They take control of their lives and, within the reality that there are some things we can't control, forge ahead with resolve. A friend of mine summed up that philosophy of life—which happened to be his own—with a Latin phrase on the bottom of his stationery. Translated, it read: "Drive it like you owned it." That's what successful people do.

Am I Always Prepared?

The concept we discussed earlier of rehearsing for a job interview is one that should be remembered throughout our working lives. Successful people try to anticipate problems and mentally prepare themselves to handle them. They don't walk into a meeting that's been scheduled for a week and ad-lib their way through their presentation. They have rehearsed it, perhaps using a tape recorder, and have written down every major question that they can imagine will arise. They are aware of the need to communicate clearly and with enthusiasm if an idea is to have a chance of being accepted. So many good ideas fail to be acted upon because they were presented inadequately. The ability to communicate (as the studies at the beginning of this chapter show) is crucial to success, not only in business but in our everyday life. Relationships suffer when what's on the mind of one party is misunderstood because it was not presented clearly. If you are uncomfortable communicating your ideas, take steps to correct it. Attend a night course in expository writing. Take a similar course in public speaking.

Practice. Rehearse. *Prepare yourself for success.*

The world is filled with people who simply shrug and say, "That's the way I am."

Nonsense. With few exceptions, each of us can change aspects of our personality for the better. Changing ourselves takes hard work, but the result is certainly worth it. We feel better about ourselves. Our lives take on a renewed richness and purpose. And, ultimately, we become successful.

It's up to *each of us* to develop an attitude for success.

No one can do it for us.

8

ONWARD AND UPWARD

Use your head to get ahead.

At this point, a pattern should be emerging where finding success in data processing is concerned. From the very beginning—deciding what career path to take, looking for available jobs, preparing a résumé, rehearsing for the interview, and now taking stock of your attitudes for success—it has been the *intangible* factors that played the most prevalent roles.

No matter how technically prepared you are for the data-processing field, you'll have to look beyond that preparation if you are to achieve true success.

A survey recently reported in Dow Jones's *National Business Employment Weekly* indicates that of all the factors directly relating to employee advancement, getting exposure was considered most important by 60 percent of those surveyed. Thirty percent felt that image was the crucial ingredient, and only 10 percent pointed to job performance.

A literal reading of this would lead you to believe that you don't have to know your job or perform it in order to get ahead.

We know this isn't what the study intended. Don't do your job and not only will you fail to achieve success, but you will be fired.

Every data processor knows the importance of doing an effective job, and most work hard at it. The point made by the above survey—and hundreds of others that touch on similar subjects—is that of the hundreds performing well at their data-processing jobs, only a few will make a smooth and timely advance through the ranks to higher positions. Technical knowledge and performance are not questioned by top management. They are expected. What sets those few achievers apart from the others is, as the survey indicates, exposure and image, along with other intangible factors to which this chapter is devoted.

Let's take the matter of exposure. I have written countless columns and given numerous interviews on the subject of exposure because its importance is beyond debate. What do we mean by "exposure"? When you were looking for a job, you obviously weren't going to find one unless people knew about you and that you were available. You used your network to get the word out. You called friends, and friends of friends, and you sent letters not only in response to want ads in the newspapers and trade magazines, but to companies that had not advertised a job but for whom you felt you'd be interested in working. You gained exposure for yourself.

But once you have landed a job, there is a tendency to submerge yourself in it and to ignore the need to continue actively seeking the sort of exposure within your company and industry that could lead to bigger and better things.

Here are some ways to prevent this.

Within the Company

Good companies usually prefer to promote from within. This is not an altruistic policy. Rather, it reflects good business sense. An employee who has been with the company for a period of time is a known entity. Hiring an outsider, whose credentials may not be what the résumé promises, or whose attitude may not fit in with the company's culture, is far riskier than promoting their own people. What that means to you— no matter what level of data processing you are func- tioning at in the company—is that unless you make upper management aware of your existence, your tal- ents, and your ambition, promotions will be slow to come.

Company Publications

People who edit company publications are always looking for news that would be of interest to all employees. One of their biggest complaints—and I've discussed this with a number of them—is the general reluctance of employees to recognize that something they have done is newsworthy and to bring it to the editor's attention. Many of us are reluctant to seek publicity for ourselves, because we feel it smacks of egotism. It doesn't, and we do a service not only to the editor and to the company but to ourselves as well when we make known an interesting project we are working on, or some significant event in our lives that would interest others. If going after solo publicity bothers you, look for ways to include it in what your department is doing. If you play a significant role in a successful departmental project, you will naturally be mentioned in whatever is written about it. Not only that, but everyone with whom you work will enjoy having their efforts recognized in print.

Another approach would be to offer to write a monthly column about your department and its people for a company publication. A number of people from our network of offices contribute such columns to *Half-Times*, an in-house monthly publication that goes to everyone in the organization. Not only does this bring them to the attention of their peers, but the thoughts and ideas expressed in their columns provide useful information to others performing the same job.

There's another benefit, besides exposure, to becoming involved with company publications, and that's the opportunity to sharpen your written-communication skills. If they are woefully lacking, it might be an incentive to take a course in clear, expository writing, which you'll use to advantage throughout your working life. Being able to distinctly express an idea or process on paper is one of the most valuable tools anyone seeking success can possess.

Offer to Help

No matter how familiar with personal computers just about everyone in business is today, there is a tendency on the part of those not directly related to data processing to be suspicious of it and at times scornful of its role. Why? We tend to distrust anything we don't understand.

When I asked in a Burke study what complaints top management had about their DP departments, these were some actual responses:

"They think they're a cure-all."

"Too aloof."

"The inability to communicate in everyday language."

"They are not aware and don't focus on the company's mission. The focus is on data processing and not what the company is doing."

"Inability to see issues from a top management perspective."

"Data processors are not in the mainstream."

"DP people think that the computer is more important than the company itself."

"Not relating to people and interacting with people."

What these attitudes create for you, a data processor, is the opportunity to turn them around through education. Once you have established yourself in your job, you might offer to hold a once-a-week evening seminar on computers and their contribution to the company. Another approach you could take is to offer the same sort of evening class on how computers work, particularly personal computers and how they can contribute to every person's daily life. Obviously, there are other subjects you could cover on a volunteer basis in such a class. Your involvement in offering and conducting such seminars not only provides a service to others in the company, but also accomplishes what you've set out to do—gain wider exposure for yourself outside your immediate department and outside your company.

Another possible activity along these lines occurs when a department within the company is about to have a new or improved computer system installed. Again, the prevailing attitude on the part of noncomputer people is to resist the change. This resistance stems from not knowing much about computers and having been denied access to that knowledge because of the tendency of data-processing people to surround it with technical jargon and mystique. If your department is engaged in implementing a new computer system for, let's say, the records department of a hospital, you can offer to act as liaison between your technical people and those who will be end users—the record-keeping clerks. You can offer to hold meetings with them at which the new system and how they will ultimately benefit from it are explained in lay terms.

An important word of advice here about these kinds of activities: explain the computer system in understandable language and concepts. I remember once speaking to an experienced private pilot who was angry at the tendency of other pilots to show off when

they took up for a ride someone who was not experienced in aviation, and who was naturally apprehensive
about flying in a small plane. Instead of allaying their
fears by giving them a smooth, uneventful flight, these
pilots would deliberately put the plane through its
paces in order to impress their passenger. Of course,
the exact opposite effect was the result.

The same idea holds true when communicating your
technical expertise to those outside the data-processing
field. Keep it simple, and leave the technical phrases and
words back in the DP department. Following that bit of
advice could enhance your career potential, according
to another study we conducted in data processing. We
asked DP management and top management whether, in
their judgment, data processors who communicate and
articulate well find it much easier to get ahead. The
response was a resounding "Yes!" Ninety-six percent of
the respondents agreed, with only 1 percent disagreeing,
and 3 percent remaining neutral.

Be Sociable

Because the personality of the DPer has tended to be
more withdrawn than expansive, the social opportunities offered by a company are too often ignored. Becoming a part of your company's social structure
doesn't mean that you have to become a social nui-
sance. It does suggest that planned social events for the
purpose of bringing employees together are a good
opportunity not only to extend your exposure within
the company, but to offer your ideas in a relaxed

setting. As much as you may try to resist the notion that in order to advance in a company you must play the social "game," the stark reality is that it's expected of you. Companies function best when their employees get along, and one way to foster this is to periodically bring them together outside of the workaday environment. The loner, no matter how skilled a data processor, is soon treated that way, not only socially but where plans for promotions are concerned. "I do my job; that should be enough" is a philosophy that will stand in your way in today's corporate climate. Yes, you must do your job, but it is not enough.

One of the reasons some data processors shun social events is that they have become so immersed in their world of computers, terminals, and programs that they have failed to develop social skills. These people tend to want to talk only to others who share that same limited interest. A good data processor is valuable to a company. A good data processor with wider interests is even more valuable. By all means share social times with your peers, but if you aspire to move up in the corporate structure, get used to conversing and socializing with people who really don't want to talk about your technical specialty.

Within the Industry

In effect, every data processor has two industries to consider when looking for increased exposure. The first, of course, is data processing itself. The second is the industry in which the company competes.

For example, if you are a programmer with a large bank, you can seek exposure through data-processing trade journals and organizations as well as through groups and publications within the banking industry. Obviously, taking advantage of both opportunities broadens your scope and gives you a double chance to promote yourself.

There seems to be at least one trade journal for every pursuit, and the popular professions and occupations spawn a number of them. Like the editors of company newsletters, trade journal editors are constantly on the lookout for material. It isn't easy putting out a monthly publication about a single discipline, and people who approach them with ideas and articles are welcome.

There is nothing more impressive to a potential new employer than a person who has been "published." We've all heard the term "publish or perish," which is generally applied to the academic world. Professors who are not published in leading scholarly journals find themselves falling behind when it comes to advancement within the academic ranks. The same might not be so literally true for other professions, but there is a lesson to be learned. Recognition outside your own company carries with it an image of achievement that can't fail to impress your boss or the person you approach for your next job in data processing.

Again, it comes down to becoming comfortable with the written word, and I urge you to use whatever educational opportunities are available to sharpen your writing skills. The demands of writing for trade journals are not so stringent that only those about to write the great American novel need apply. Far from it; good ideas and projects written about with some sense of clarity and order will be turned into a publishable piece by the editors. That doesn't mean that you can turn in sloppy work. Any submission to a trade magazine should be typewritten (or written on a word processor), double-spaced, and should incorporate very basic writing skills. If some of the grammar, syntax, and punctuation is off, those are the kinds of things an editor will correct.

Some companies have a policy that employees writing for outside publications must clear the material through their supervisor. This is the exception rather than the rule, however. The impact of having your boss pick up a leading trade journal and see an article written by you is significant. It establishes you as a recognizable person within the *broad* field of data processing.

Community Activities

There are opportunities for you to share your knowledge of computers with the community at large. If such opportunities don't seem readily available, you can create them. A religious or civic organization might be interested in having you lecture or conduct courses in basic computer knowledge for underprivileged children, or for adults looking to gain insight into computers that they can apply on their jobs. Local schools welcome guest speakers; you could introduce the world of computers and business to youngsters. The local community newspaper, always looking for interesting topics, might entertain the notion of having you write a column about the use of computers in banking, or retailing, or whatever industry you're presently in. It comes back to the concept of being active, not only within your company, but outside it. Many community activities attract the attention of the local press, which, like an article in a trade journal, can't fail to impress your boss with your initiative and knowledge.

The data processor who is willing and able to take the highly complex world of computers and present it in an understandable and palatable manner to the community in general is a valuable commodity. The company for which you work gains recognition, the veil of mystery that surrounds computing is penetrated, and you gain a significant measure of respect. In effect, you are functioning as your own public relations counselor, and good public relations is always valuable for someone looking to achieve success.

9
STRATEGY FOR SUCCESS

You can make yourself luckier.

We've talked about the necessity of having the right *attitude* for success. Now let's turn to having the right *strategy*.

Once you're entrenched in data processing and have had, through experience and exposure, the opportunity to see yourself and the industry in a broader perspective, it's time to begin evaluating career goals and the steps that will enable you to reach them.

In a sense, we're going back to a more tangible, cognitive approach to your career now. We're talking about doing some hard thinking, which, hopefully, will help you make the right career decisions.

First, don't be afraid to make a move, either within your company or outside it. The fear of failure and rejection causes many people to avoid going after something worthwhile. If that's part of your psychological makeup, work at shedding it. Successful people are not afraid to make a move once they have taken advantage of all available input in their decision-making process. Where are the best opportunities in data processing for you? What aspects of the industry look as if they will grow in the coming years? What jobs have you found most pleasing, and how can your experience to date be best utilized? How high do you ultimately want to climb, and what are the best roads leading to that position? Once you have answered these questions, and a host of others that will come to you, you are in a position to take action on the answers.

Timing Plays a Role

By timing, I'm not talking about being in the right place at the right time, although that does occasionally pay off for a small percentage of people. Instead, I mean timing your decisions and actions.

Men and women who have successfully navigated the waters (more often rapids and heavy surf) of data processing have been helped by a developed sense of *when* to make a career move. Many others fail to do this and lose the opportunity for advancement.

For example, many bright young programmers or software engineers begin their career with a bang. Their work is exemplary and they are in a company that rewards them with periodic and sizable raises.

That sounds good, of course, and it is, if these people stop at some point and weigh the next raise against making a vertical move to another plateau such as systems analyst, or moving into a position of senior software engineer.

No one can tell you when that decision should be made. In fact, no one can tell you what your decision should be when you reach that point. The salient principle here is that you should be aware that in most careers there might come a time to leave a comfortable, rewarding job for one that may not work out as well, but that offers possible growth. That risk has to be balanced with the reality that if you *don't* make that move, you may be unwilling to do it a few years down the road.

Of course, this can happen to anyone at any level of data processing. Someone who has risen to a position of project leadership, perhaps after ten years in the field, sees the next career move to, perhaps, first- or second-line management. Being a project leader is a position of authority and responsibility, and carries with it generally impressive financial compensation. Do you continue in your present position and stay with it for the rest of your data-processing career, or do you take a chance and risk it all for potentially greater rewards?

People face this kind of decision in every walk of life. Game-show contestants very often are called upon to gamble what they've already won in order to win more.

Airline pilots are another example. When the Boeing 747 jumbo jet was introduced, pilots with certain major airlines who wished to upgrade from smaller aircraft to the new craft went through a period of transitional training. They were allowed to fail once and to return to their previous position as captain of a smaller jet. But if they failed a second time, it was the end of their career. Commanding a 747 paid significantly more money than did the same position with 707s and 727s, but reaching for the higher rung was fraught with peril.

Successful vice-presidents in large corporations are often lured by headhunters into accepting the presidency of a smaller, riskier company. Actors and actresses often must decide whether to leave the security of a long-running television series to take a more challenging and iffy role on Broadway.

The list goes on. Everyone is faced with these decisions at various times in their career, and they are decisions that should be carefully weighed.

The question of *job hopping* often comes up here. It poses less of a problem and carries less stigma than it did years ago, when someone was expected to find a job and stay with the company until retirement. Today's educated and skilled young data processors see frequent job change as the fast track toward bigger and better jobs, higher salaries, and keeping up with the state of the art. Studies peg turnover for systems analysts and programmers at between 10 and 20 percent. It's not unusual these days to run into people in data processing who have had ten or twelve jobs over a fifteen-year stretch.

Does it hurt you to have switched jobs often? It depends upon who is in the position to hire you next. Some managers are highly skeptical of people who have jumped from job to job, but a lot depends upon that employer's corporate culture and upon the nature of its business. A large, monolithic organization will prize job stability far more than a smaller, more dynamic shop where turnover represents an influx of new ideas and energy. DPers who have worked in a variety of settings have amassed broad knowledge, which can benefit a new employer.

On the flip side of the coin, losing data processors after training them costs money, to say nothing of the turmoil it creates within a department. When everything is taken into consideration, industry estimates of what it costs a company to lose a good DPer after only a year on the job run anywhere between $20,000 and $40,000. Suffer enough of these losses and it's understandable why companies look for people who will stay around awhile.

Hiring professionals apply one basic rule to the question of whether someone has changed jobs too often, and that's whether each change represented a step up into a better position, more responsibility and challenge, and higher pay. If they haven't, it's assumed that the frequent changes reflect basic instability in the individual, rather than having an eye out for opportunity.

For some reason, many people equate advancement with leaving a job. It doesn't have to be that way, not if you are open to the potentials within your current organization and adopt the attitude of constantly being "interviewed" for that better inside job. If those potentials truly aren't there, then by all means look to other companies.

Forecasting the Future

If you could accurately predict the future, you wouldn't be bothered reading a book about achieving success in any field. Still—largely because of computers—we are able to make assessments of what various future trends might be, based upon the ability to gather and codify large amounts of data.

According to the best projections available through 1995, the largest increase in jobs will take place in such fields as medical services, business services, computers and peripheral equipment, transportation, professional services, scientific instruments, communications, and plastic products. Here we're talking *industry*, not specifically data processing—but if you recall the statistics presented in the introduction and first chapter of this book, *all* industry in the future will have as its base some form of data processing. Therefore, if you are trying to analyze future industries that could afford you the best opportunity for growth and advancement, you might consider those I have just mentioned.

However, that doesn't mean that you should give up on an industry in which you have a particular interest in order to enhance your chances of success. Many naturally gifted teachers were dissuaded from entering the profession a few years ago because it was overcrowded. They ended up in other fields that probably did make them more money, but the teaching profession lost needed talent, and the chances are that these people never really found happiness in their other career choices. While I heartily recommend thinking about those business areas that offer a bright future, I must fall back on my basic thesis that people with the right attitude and strategy for success will achieve their goals in virtually whatever they set out to do. Besides, along with career success, we have an obligation to ourselves to find happiness and fulfillment in our lives.

Industry groups aside, there are significant changes occurring within data processing itself that might be worth thinking about.

For instance, there is a definite move toward developing data-processing *generalists*. The reason is simple: companies have found that they need to overstaff their data-processing departments in order to have on hand a wide variety of skills to handle peak loads. This is expensive. When skilled employees spend a great deal of time on the job doing nothing or very little, they get bored and leave. That reality forces companies not only to overstaff, but to pay high salaries in an attempt to keep their DPers happy.

A more cost-effective solution is now being pursued, which is to develop selected individuals into data processors with a wide range of skills, and to pay accordingly for their increased value to a company. That's why it is so important to be continually seeking out new avenues of education and experience within the broad spectrum of data processing.

Another trend in data processing is the increased focus on managing of information within an organization. One of the keys to any company's success is the ability to create, assimilate, produce, and distribute timely information. With the advent and growth of desktop publishing, more and more information is being generated and produced in-house, and individuals who are able to create systems through which the flow of information can be expedited will be in demand.

Anyone who can add to his or her title the term "telecommunications" will enjoy increased demand and opportunity over the next ten years. As management in every industry looks to cut labor costs, the use of automated equipment to service customer needs will increase proportionately. Banks are a good example; the growth of ATMs (automatic teller machines) is well documented, and the move toward increasing this approach to labor saving shows a distinct upward trend. Wherever the technology of the computer age can be applied, the need for talented and skilled personnel to create the systems and make them work is enhanced.

Computer security is another growth area in data processing that will need a large number of new people in coming years. The theft of information from computer systems has become of paramount importance to governments and private industry alike, and huge sums are being spent to secure data-processing operations.

Most significant for you to remember is that as our entire industrial base becomes more dependent upon computer technology, the importance of people like yourself increases in every area of data processing. The move toward totally automated offices and factories is like a steamroller in our society, and those who ride with it are the individuals who are constantly looking in the direction of its progress and preparing for the next stop on its journey.

There are other things every data processor should be thinking about when pondering a future in data processing. Some of them are:

• *Keep up with the field.* Achievers in any field find the time and expend the effort to keep current with what's going on, not only as it applies to their specific jobs but as it affects their industry as a whole. Data processing has given birth to numerous trade publications, and you should at least make it a point to read the relevant ones each month.

• *Keep learning.* Learning is a lifetime pursuit. At least, it should be. Because of the maze of technology in data processing, it takes extra effort to keep up with state-of-the-art concepts. But it must be done to prevent falling behind. At the same time—and based upon the sort of data presented in this book, which indicate that successful DPers in the future will have to become proficient at written and verbal communication—educational avenues to prepare you for these noncomputer skills must be pursued, too. Acquiring communication skills doesn't have to represent a long-term commitment in the way that data processing does. Proficient writing is a learned craft and should be viewed that way. Your goal should be to create clear and succinct business correspondence. Once you have learned the craft of writing (and, possibly, have taken some courses in public speaking, so that you're comfortable making verbal presentations, too), the skills are maintained and sharpened by doing, and by incorporating writing and speaking into your daily activities.

"Insuring" Your Career

We insure our homes and cars and lives, but never stop to think of the necessity to insure our careers. I don't know of an insurance company who will offer such coverage, but there are things we can do to provide our own career insurance.

All of the things I've mentioned so far—keeping abreast of the field and its technology, learning to communicate better, building and maintaining our network of contacts—help insure our future market-ability. But there's more we can do to provide work "insurance" throughout our lives.

Anyone with a knowledge of data processing is in a good position to develop a part-time business. It doesn't have to be so consuming that it interferes with your primary job, but it can be nurtured to the point where it can provide a measure of security should you find yourself without employment for any period of time. Even the best of us are sometimes the victim of industry forces beyond our control, and having a part-time business to fall back upon can make a big difference in our finances. Not only that: by slowly developing our own business during off time, we expand our network of contacts, add to our experience and knowledge, and, in general, fund our own job insurance.

The whole question of moonlighting for DPers is wrapped up in the larger question of business ethics. Let's take a look at that question from a DPer's perspective.

Anyone with a full-time DP job who uses company time to work on part-time activities, or who uses supplies or company technology for them, is engaged in unethical and unlawful behavior, and there is no excuse for it. Any company issuing you a paycheck deserves your full loyalty and attention during working hours. The same holds true for permanently employed data processors who use their spare time to do work for a competitor.

On the other hand, there are apparent advantages for an employer when a valuable permanent employee develops an ongoing outside business interest using his or her data-processing knowledge. As studies indicate, people attracted to the data-processing field have a great need for challenge and growth. Often, as data-processing departments become more standardized and bureaucratic, the employer finds it difficult to provide those challenges, and outside business activities by their employees can do it for them.

Another benefit of such activity to the permanent employer is the outlet it provides for good DP employees. Most people's hobbies have nothing to do with their jobs. For many data processors, computers *are* their hobby, and encouraging them to engage in it provides a psychological lift and, by extension, increased knowledge that can be applied to the permanent job.

There are many ways to apply data-processing

knowledge in a moonlighting situation. Some of the ideas on how to gain exposure apply here. Many small businesses need consultants who can help them make maximum use of whatever computer systems they've installed, and are more than happy to pay someone on a contract basis.

Those of you with PCs at home can develop businesses utilizing the capabilities of your equipment. For example, you can offer word-processing services, computer graphics for local artists and printers, and electronic spreadsheet services for accounting firms.

If you should decide to pursue a moonlighting venture as a means of insuring your income, don't feel you're doing something out of the ordinary. A recent issue of *U.S. News & World Report* notes that between 1975 and 1985 the percentage of white-collar workers with more than one income rose from 4 percent to 5.4 percent. Among the nation's 105 million workers there are more than 5 million moonlighters. It is no longer true that moonlighters are primarily blue-collar workers taking menial second jobs to make ends meet. The growth in moonlighting is with professional and technical people, like yourself. The same holds true for jobs available through temporary-employment services. At Accountemps, most of the people we provide to clients on a temporary basis are highly skilled and have considerable knowledge of their areas of specialization.

A word of advice if you should decide to moonlight: tell your employer about it. Present it in all its positive light and with your assurance that it will in no way interfere with your primary responsibility to the company. Some firms have specific restrictions against moonlighting, and to deliberately ignore them without prior permission is to jeopardize your primary source of income. If that happens, instead of insuring your income you've made sure your primary source will cease.

Ethics and Loyalty

Information management professionals must show themselves as basically decent human beings—not anonymous techies. We must be ourselves—people who are honest, ethical, and concerned with the public good.

And we should not only be honest and ethical, we should be known to be so.

The above is taken from a letter written by David R. Smith, international president of the Data Processing Management Association (DPMA). It touches upon a subject that concerns all of us in our personal and professional lives, and that should be carefully considered by each of you reading this book.

The question of business ethics has been with us since the very beginning. Every industry and company is occasionally faced with conduct by an employee that even under the most generous of definitions would have to be considered unethical. The field of data processing is not different, but because of its unique impact upon the lives of everyone, it offers a fertile field for unethical behavior.

The increasing emphasis upon security in data processing hasn't happened by accident. It is supply and demand at its best. As cases of unethical behavior by DPers increase, the need to police these activities expands at a parallel rate.

Professional organizations within data processing have been addressing this problem through analysis of it, and by attempting to draw professional guidelines to represent a standard of ethical behavior in the field. The subject of business ethics is grist for a book unto itself, but it does seem worth mentioning here, if only to raise the consciousness of each of you striving for a successful career in data processing.

It would behoove you to spend some time thinking about the ethics of data processing, and assuring yourself that *your* attitudes toward the use of this powerful and pervasive force in our society are in line with basic ethical principles.

Of course, there is a whole range of business ethics that is not unique to data processing. The way we conduct ourselves in our daily business lives, no matter what the field, will play a significant role in determining just how far we advance. Usually, the question of whether an act is ethical or unethical involves seemingly small things. For instance, the frequent use of a company copying machine to make personal copies is unethical, to say nothing of being unfair. Using a company phone for excessive personal calls, stealing time from the workday for personal chores, badmouthing your company to a competitor, and a whole range of other "insignificant" actions are, in fact, unethical.

A good example is how certain individuals handle the search for a new job. It is my contention that no employee, at any level, has a right to discuss job changing while in the company office and on company time. It not only is not fair to the company paying their salary, it's *unethical*, and could cost them their job at an inconvenient time. This situation often arises when a headhunter contacts an employee to see whether that person would be interested in changing jobs. The ethical response is to get the individual's name and number and arrange to talk after business hours. The unethical way to handle this is to close your office door and engage in a conversation that obviously contributes nothing to your company's productivity, and that also is an act of disloyalty. It has nothing to do with whether you wish to change jobs. That is your decision and you have a perfect right to make it. Rather, it involves the way you go about it, a philosophy summed up in the old song from the swing era, " 'Tain't Whacha Do, 'Tis the Way Howcha Do It." Running many personal copies on an idle company copying machine after asking permission to do so is ethical. Doing it surreptitiously is unethical.

I firmly believe, and have practiced throughout my business career, that ethical behavior is not only *right*, but also pays off for the individual or company practicing it. A short-term profit gained by sacrificing good business practices invariably results in a long-term loss. The foundation of a successful career depends upon a commitment to ethics; ethics is an ingredient of professionalism; ethical people have little fear of disobeying the law.

An afterthought about dealing with headhunters who seek you out. That can be a stimulating experience. It certainly tends to boost one's ego. The problem is that headhunters sometimes do not actually represent any company looking for someone with your qualifications and could be using you as a basis for soliciting an assignment. If you are happy with your job, and not particularly interested in leaving, do you really want to allow yourself to become their bait? Are you sure it won't get back to your present employer? How did the headhunter happen to find you? Ask for names and details before taking that next step, no matter how ego-boosting it may be.

10

MIND OVER MATTER

*If you can program your mind you can
program your success.*

Finding your first job in data processing may have
taken hard work, and pursuing your maximum potential in the field takes a great deal more effort.

But what about the thing that occupies most of your
time between that entry-level job and a $200,000 a year
slot in MIS? That time is taken up with performing, to
the best of your capabilities, whatever job you are
currently holding down.

Your future success depends to a great extent upon
your performance at various DP jobs along the way,
Everyone, employed in any field, is faced with the
daily problem of pleasing a boss, interacting with
fellow workers, organizing a workday, seeking recognition and rewards for a job well done, and coping with
the inherent stress of a busy professional life. Let's deal
with stress on the job first, beginning with the general
stress experienced by all people in the business world.

We often create our own stress on the job. That doesn't represent just a thought of mine. It's the consensus of many experts who study occupational stress. It comes down to the concept of controlling our lives, rather than having external forces take control over us.

But what about those external forces that are a reality of most jobs and will be present no matter what we do—things like deadlines, unreasonable demands from superiors and clients, equipment that isn't up to the task we've been given, and all the other situations that create anxiety and tension?

The answer doesn't rest in changing the externals. Instead, it involves the way we react to those forces.

For example, a programmer is given an impossible deadline to meet and knows that finishing the job on time will mean many nights and weekends of work. That in itself is stressful, but added to it is the fact that the boss is the type of individual who only criticizes and never praises, and the programmer's spouse is going to react negatively to the prolonged disruption of family life.

Here are some things you can do in this situation to ease the stress.

First, deal with the personal component of the problem. Sit down with your spouse and explain the situation. Admit your fear that the reaction at home is contributing to what is already a stressful situation, and suggest that you work out a schedule that will allow you to do your job to the best of your ability and at the same time recognize your need to spend time with your family. This specific suggestion is not nearly so important as what's behind it—that people who are damaged most by stress are those who refuse to acknowledge the pressure they're under and won't openly seek to discuss it with those involved. It's a classic situation: a household is disrupted because one of the partners in it carries home the burden of the job and, instead of admitting it, keeps it inside and creates a situation that only gets worse as time goes on. Victims of stress (victims in the sense that their marriage falls apart or health suffers) are those who consider admitting the need for help to be a sign of weakness. It's a sign of strength, of course, and those who see it from that perspective manage to cope with job-related stress more successfully.

The notion of discussing the stress you are under carries through to the job as well. Perhaps the deadline set by your boss is so impossible that the only result will be failure. Simply waiting for the day when the failure will become apparent—deadline day—only increases the tension placed upon you. People who are secure in their jobs and in themselves are not afraid to tell a superior that the deadline for a given job can't be met, and will offer alternative suggestions. I'm not talking about finding excuses for not getting a job done. Employees who do that don't get away with it very often and find their career advancement stymied, as it should be.

Instead, I'm suggesting that if you have given a task your full attention, have considered all the possible means of accomplishing it, and, despite all the resources at your fingertips, are convinced that it can't be done in the time demanded, you should state your position and continue to seek alternative ways of accomplishing the mission.

The boss I mentioned earlier—the one who only criticizes and never praises—might be the sort of person who will not tolerate that kind of realistic evaluation of a project. In that case, you have two choices: either to quit or to decide that you will do everything in your power to accommodate that boss. Either choice brings its own brand of stress. Either you're out of work, or you're facing a grueling schedule. What then?

You have smoothed things over at home by having worked out some way of still being part of the family. Maybe that involved setting up a schedule of time together instead of simply allowing weeks to slip by in the hope that things will ease up. It could be a matter of reserving one night a week for dinner together or taking a weekend out of the hectic work schedule to do something you have both wanted to do very much.

Now you turn to the job at hand—completing the project as close to deadline as possible.

Become superorganized. Disorganized people suffer the most stress because things seem overwhelming to them. Take time to clear your desk of everything except the important project. Some people find that by sitting at another desk, preferably in another office, they are subjected to far less distraction and are able to concentrate on the project. Use time when you are exhausted and unable to concentrate to get rid of more routine, mundane matters. Use your most alert and rested time to attack the big challenge.

Recognize that breaks in the day do not take away from your productivity. Instead, they contribute to it. Make it a rule during this intense period not to have a sandwich at your desk for lunch. Get out of the office and take a walk, change your surroundings, do anything to break the stressful monotony of the project. Even leaving your office and working in an empty conference room for an hour or two can do wonders for your spirits. It is when a project presses down on us like a heavy gray cloud that the pressure begins to build and the resultant stress grows to unhealthy levels.

Don't ignore the need for regular exercise. Doing something physical does wonders for the mind and raises the overall energy level. Even if it involves ten-minute breaks at your desk to do some isometric exercises, take the time. You will more than make it up in increased productivity.

Be aware that simply putting in time does not represent progress toward the completion of the project. Be honest enough with yourself to know that on a given night, taking home three or four hours of work is ultimately going to be counterproductive. You will lose that time with your family, and the effort you put into the work you hauled home will contribute little to the project's completion.

Ask for help. Go to your boss (as difficult as he or she might be) and state clearly your reasons for needing additional help. If that fails, ask your boss if you can call upon some of your colleagues within the data-processing department to get the help you need. (You can always offer to return the favor when your workload has slackened and the other person is faced with the same sort of deadline.)

Besides these specific approaches, the most important thing you can do is to analyze yourself and the reason why stress caused by this project is taking an unusually high toll on you. It could be that you are experiencing undue fear of the ramifications if the project is not finished to perfection precisely on the day it was called for. A serious illness is something to fear; an occasional failure on the job is not. If you fail with this project because you haven't applied yourself, and haven't used every resource available to you, you have some reason to fear the consequences. However, if you have given it *everything you have,* there's nothing to be ashamed of . . . and nothing to fear.

This concept of how we tend to exaggerate our fears in business is well known to industrial psychologists and has a great deal to do with the way we view ourselves. Let's take an example of this.

You are a bright, educated, skilled, experienced, and hardworking programmer in a large company. You do a good job because you have the skills and you are motivated. Still, when your boss calls and asks you to come to her office at four o'clock to discuss something important, your mind immediately assumes the worst. You are going to be reprimanded for something or be asked about your current project and not have the right answers. The list of imagined scenarios goes on, and by the time you reach the four o'clock meeting, stress has turned you into a quivering mass of fear, which is sure to make your performance at the meeting a disaster.

Instead, considering your attributes, you might have

countered those negative thoughts with some logical thinking. If you are to be called on the carpet for something you've done in the past, that isn't a matter of life or death. You know that you're good, and that you work hard, and even if there is something negative to be brought up, it doesn't mean you will be told to clean out your desk and be gone by five. By the same token, there's no disgrace in not having some answers on the tip of your tongue for every question asked by a superior. In fact, one of the most appealing attributes of anyone in business is the ability to say "I don't know, but I'll get the answer for you."

By changing the way we view ourselves and by reevaluating the importance of most events in our working day, we can virtually eliminate free-floating stress from our business lives.

But we don't want to eliminate *all* stress. If we did that, we wouldn't function very well as interested, striving human beings. Ask any performer whether they feel nervous before going onstage and they will invariably say, "Of course I do. If I didn't, there would be something wrong with me."

A certain amount of stress is healthy and productive. It keeps us on our toes and reminds us that we have to be prepared for what happens in our daily lives. Stress, a healthy amount of it, is the fuel for pushing beyond our normal boundaries and accomplishing things we thought we weren't capable of accomplishing. It gives us a competitive edge, picks us up when our spirits are down, and propels us toward the next goal in our lives. But, like everything else, it's a matter of balance. Stress might be natural and normal, but we must make use of it to benefit ourselves, rather than allowing it to destroy us.

The computer age has created its own peculiar forms of anxiety and stress. It has even spawned its own medical term—"cyberphobia"—which is used to describe people's adverse reactions to computers. Interestingly enough, those suffering from cyberphobia are more likely than not to be out of the mainstream of data processing. These are the people in your company who are aware that they are becoming more and more dependent upon computer technology, yet so distrust and fear computers that they are capable of generating a whole set of physical symptoms in them. These people need data processors in their companies who, rather than continuing to build mystique about computers, devote themselves to simplifying the subject. Maybe in future years there will be a new data-processing occupation, *computer therapists*.

Computer anxiety is not reserved for the noncomputer person, however. The nature of data processing has built-in sources of tension. Even the most gregarious data processors will spend a great deal of time interacting one-on-one with a computer rather than with other people. While this may be acceptable to those who are naturally introverted, it takes a toll on most people over a long period of time. That's why it is so important for you to seek opportunities to mingle with people instead of just with machines. Not only is it good for your career advancement, but it's good for your mental health as well.

Deadlines, mentioned earlier, can be particularly difficult for data processors to meet because management establishing the deadlines often has little knowledge of or interest in what goes into the creation of a system and the software to make it work. This can raise frustration levels in DPers to jarring proportions, and it takes constant effort not to let it influence your attitude toward those making what seem to be unreasonable demands or to allow it to interfere with your work on the project. Here again is a wonderful opportunity for an ongoing educational process to take place within a company, led by men and women in data processing who recognize the benefits to be derived from bringing the department more into the mainstream of company objectives and policies.

Don't be the private pilot who needs to show off to a first-time passenger the technical capabilities of a plane and, in the process, loses a potential advocate of private aviation. Successful DPers know that the machine is not as important as what it can do for end users—*people*. A sophisticated airplane should be used to transport people smoothly, safely, and without incident from one place to another. The same holds true for computers. They should carry a company's business objectives through a maze of problems to a satisfactory and profitable conclusion.

Burnout

"Burning out," at least according to Webster, is: "to burn till the fuel is exhausted and the fire ceases."

The reason it is so important to combat the effects of stress is to avoid reaching the point where our fuel is exhausted and the fire inside us ceases to burn. It can happen; stress takes a remarkable toll on the body. For instance, it's estimated that 60 percent of all visits to physicians are for stress-related illnesses. We're all aware of the epidemic of illegal narcotics in our country, but the three most commonly used drugs are still tranquilizers, hypertension medications, and medicines for ulcers. Air traffic controllers, who are constantly under tension on the job, actually have a section on their attendance record that reads: "Day off—On pills."

Various studies peg the loss of productivity and out-of-pocket expenses to American business because of stress at as much as $75 billion per year.

"Burnout" has become a fashionable new word in our vocabulary. Like so many other things in our society, it is simply a new and different way of explaining what workers have felt for ages—the adverse effects of prolonged periods of hard work. Fatigue. Being tired and ready for a vacation. The problem, from my point of view, with the term "burnout" is that it has become almost fashionable to claim being burned out. I wish it hadn't taken on that meaning, because it tends to confuse the much larger issue of work-related stress and in too many cases has given employees the opportunity to *cop out*, using burnout as an excuse.

Still, there can be little debate that those who do not take steps to deal with stress on the job will become part of the 60 percent of those Americans making appointments to see their physicians.

Researchers who study the effects of stress on data processors all report an increase in the incidence of stress-induced illness, and because the growth of the computer industry is a fact of our modern life, the damage to the bright and talented continues to mount. Sadly, so-called burnout affects the best and the brightest, the most ambitious and hardworking, the very people you don't expect it from and most hope will not fall victim to it. Victims of occupational stress are people who take their jobs and careers seriously, who will make great sacrifices to accomplish a project, and who are often the bright stars with the most promising futures ahead of them.

One of the reasons stress is particularly prevalent in data processing is that, according to experts in the field, a sense of loss of control is at the root of all occupational stress. Younger professionals tend to suffer more from it than do older professionals in higher positions of authority. If you take this concept and combine it with many people's feeling that *computers* have taken control of their lives, you can readily see why stress is a particularly serious problem in the data-processing field.

But, while acknowledging the effect of outside forces that create stress, this avoids the basic issue of how we react to those outside forces and what we do as individuals to guard against being unnecessarily affected by them.

Here are some symptoms you should look for in yourself to determine whether you're not doing a good job of managing the stress in your professional life.

Dr. Harry Levinson, an industrial psychologist who specializes in the area of stress, says it's time to be concerned when:

1. You feel that no matter how hard you're working, you're not getting anywhere.
2. You've developed apathy toward non-business-related activities that you once enjoyed, like golf, concerts, and getting together with friends outside of work.
3. You suffer chronic fatigue.
4. You're unduly irritable for no apparent reason.
5. A sense of being besieged has overtaken you.

Dr. Martin G. Groder, a North Carolina psychiatrist and business consultant, adds to the list:

1. You're reluctant to take on new tasks.
2. You complain more than usual, and more than necessary.
3. Renewed cycles of enthusiasm that you used to count on don't materialize as often as before.
4. You're cranky and depressed.
5. Eccentricities that weren't there before are now emerging.
6. You've developed a tendency to disassociate from office routine.

Naturally, we all suffer from one or more of these symptoms from time to time, which doesn't indicate that we are even close to being "burned out." It's when a pattern of these symptoms becomes chronic that it's time to take a close look at how we are handling ourselves under the stress of a busy and demanding data-processing job.

What can we do to combat stress in our working lives?

Techniques suggested earlier in this chapter will help. Also, change the way you *perceive* stress. Instead of viewing it as nothing but a negative force in your life, recognize that a certain amount of it is good for all of us, fuels us when the going gets tough, and helps establish priorities and deadlines in our lives that boost productivity.

Most important, don't view yourself as a *victim* of stress. That relinquishes control to it. Instead, take control of your life within the parameters of a stressful situation. Leave the office for lunch instead of eating in. Exercise. Take time to organize yourself so that it doesn't seem as though the entire world is crashing in on you. Confide in others what you're feeling because of the stress of your job and listen to suggestions. Above all, don't use stress and the fashionable buzz word "burn-out" as an excuse to wallow in self-pity. Deal with stress as a reality, and control it before it controls you.

Dealing with Frustration

Most of our working life in the computer field involves routine, repetitious, and frustrating work. I've heard lots of young people complain that their jobs are dull and that they wish they were in a "glamorous" field. The fact is that every occupation involves a significant amount of "dull"—routine—work. The difference is whether we view it as dull or see the routinized aspects of our job as not just spreadsheets and print-outs, programming language and repeated commands, but as contributing to a larger, more "glamorous" goal.

Accountants basically fall into two groups—those who see the numbers before them as only that, *numbers;* and those who see the numbers as part and parcel of a more creative end result. The same basic difference can be applied to data processors. Here is where understanding and appreciating a company's overall goals makes a big difference.

Everyone, at some stage in their career, ends up in a job that is less rewarding than they had hoped it would be. The odds are also good that we'll experience at least one boss in our lives who is not particularly sympathetic or pleasant to be with. In fact, we may well end up working for someone who is simply inefficient and inadequate to the job. That situation sets up its own particular brand of frustration and in the long run creates a mediocre data-processing department in which employee morale is low, and that falls behind the rest of the company in its growth and the esteem in which it is held.

What can you do to cope with a frustrating job and boss while making whatever moves are necessary to find a better job with a different company? Here are a few suggestions:

• Learn what role your daily work plays in the grander scheme of the department and company, and try to keep your sights on that, rather than on the tedious tasks you are called upon to perform.

• Adopt the "glass is half full, not half empty" attitude toward your job. No job is *all* bad, and those who make the best of it concentrate on its positive aspects.

• Unofficially organize a sort of self-help support group with others who share your feelings and frustrations. That doesn't mean just to complain; there's nothing more annoying than to have another person complain about a situation you're both experiencing, like two people dying of thirst in a desert and one constantly complaining about it. But learn to confide in your co-workers, and try to arrange jobs between you so that the tedium can be broken. For instance, if you are all expected to perform a repetitious task within the department, stagger schedules so that each of you has some quiet, personal time away from the tedium.

• Start adopting ways I mentioned earlier to turn a bad job into a better one. Try to rise above the mundane routine of the job and pretend that the work is much more important than it actually is. Start dressing better, as though each day represented an important opportunity. It does, if you believe in the concept of "interviewing" for a better job every day you are on the job. Even though it may seem to you—particularly if you're depressed—that no one in the company outside of your immediate group is paying attention, that seldom is the case. There are always advancement opportunities within every firm, and those who consistently put their best job-applicant face forward are often those who receive promotions.

I know a man who had distinguished himself in his

college days working for the university's campus radio station. The rule for everyone who conducted a radio show was that females were to wear skirts or dresses and men were to wear sport jackets. This person found it odd that anyone cared about what you looked like when you were on the radio. After all, no one was seeing you except others at the station. He brought up the question to the professional manager of the station and was given this answer: "This is a college station, but if you act like a college student while you're on the air, you'll sound it. If you dress up, you'll feel more mature and better about yourself, and that will come across to listeners." Adopt that attitude for a current dull, frustrating task. Dress as though you were involved in an extremely important and exciting project. Your spirits will pick up and, by extension, others in the company looking to promote from within will certainly notice your professional approach to the job.

Dealing with That Bad Boss

Your boss may be inept, a detriment to the department, and may know far less than you do, but that person is still the boss, and it's up to you to figure out a way to get along. Here are a few ideas on the subject:

• Rather than reflecting your disdain for the boss, make an effort to be supportive and to pull an even greater share of the responsibility in the department. It's good for your self-image and will impress even the most inadequate of supervisors.

• Extend your reach into other departments within the company and see where you can make a contribution. This will take extra time and effort, but it will broaden your horizons, give you a sense of not being trapped, and gain for you that important *exposure*, and ultimately it might result in a transfer and promotion without your having to leave the firm.

• Put into effect my recommendations about becoming a better communicator. Use those skills to promote yourself within the company and outside it. If you have a great deal to offer and are stymied by the dead-end nature of your present job and boss, it's up to you to do some public relations on your own behalf.

You don't have to be victimized by a job or a superior if you don't want to be. Make the best of what you have; take stock of your assets and see that others are aware of them. Rise above the situation. Those who do will pull themselves out of the quicksand of a frustrating and unpleasant job. Those who don't will find themselves sinking even deeper.

When It's Time to Leave

We leave a job for one of two reasons: either we're asked to leave or we choose to. Each carries with it its own particular set of anxieties, and each demands a different approach from us.

We talked earlier in the book about how to resign from a job. Now let's deal with the bad news, the worst-case scenario. You've been fired.

"It's the best thing that could have happened to you."

"You'll see, it will lead to something bigger and better."

"It's not the end of the world."

All of the above are true and represent the kind of reaction you're likely to receive from close friends and family. The problem is that even though eventually you will come to realize that being fired does not represent the end of the world, it's a difficult concept to grasp on to for comfort when you're going through those days right after the ax has fallen.

There are two basic lessons we can all learn from the experience of being fired. One has to do with how to handle it, and the other has to do with learning to anticipate it by reading the signs that invariably lead up to a dismissal. Let's deal with the ability to forecast it first.

Although being fired doesn't necessarily stem from any of these individual symptoms, the combination of them, particularly when exhibited over a period of time, should give you a pretty strong hint that all is not well with your position in the company. For instance:

• You start receiving a succession of memos from your boss pointing out things you haven't done, or have done poorly. Up until this point the criticisms have been verbal. Now what is probably happening is that a file is being built against you so that when it is time to dismiss you, there is documented reason for it. Every employer has to deal with the unpleasant reality of the litigious society in which we live, and employees are a lot quicker to sue over dismissal these days than they were in the past. Having a solid file to fall back on in the event of a lawsuit is very much to the employer's benefit.

• Another tip-off can be when you are no longer brought into the mainstream of the department's activities. A "silent treatment" develops, and there is a very normal reason for this. No one likes to fire somebody, and the tendency of someone who is about to do it is to avoid the individual. That brings up a good point in general about understanding the process of being fired. There are human beings in this world who actually derive pleasure from getting rid of an employee. Fortunately for mankind, those people are few and far between. Most of us dread the thought of having to tell another human being that they are losing their job and source of income. It is extremely distasteful, and human nature is such that we try to minimize the pain, maybe not so much for the person who's losing the job as for the ones who have to announce it. That's why the silent treatment often precedes breaking the news.

I can point to my own career as an example. I was once in a position that required me to dismiss a number of employees over a short period of time. I can honestly say it was one of the most depressing and difficult periods of my life, and every firing I carried out left me with a severe headache. Try to understand that your superior isn't any happier about your being fired than you are. It may be difficult to muster that sort of compassion when you get the news, but it happens to be true, and if you acknowledge it, you can adjust your attitude to make the event less damaging to your career. More about that in a moment.

• The consultants begin to arrive, and they start probing into your job. Their arrival could mean a simple attempt on the part of management to improve productivity. There's as much of a chance, however, that they are on the scene to recommend ways to cut staff (you if they focus attention upon you) and might also be looking to gain insight from you about how you do your job, to pass it on to a replacement.

• A merger or takeover occurs. Generally, employees of a smaller company that is taken over by a larger one are in the most jeopardy of losing their jobs, particularly if there is a duplication of function. Of course, there are conditions that make it impractical for the acquiring company to direct the smaller company. Ask a few questions about their corporate structure and you'll discover whether or not this is practical.

• Jobs handled by you are now going to other people in the department. Often, the excuse for this is that management has recognized that you are overworked and is trying to take the burden off you. This may be true in certain instances, but it may indicate the beginning of a process to lessen your responsibilities so that when you are ultimately dismissed, the department won't suffer as much.

• You do not figure in the company's long-term plans. Your peers begin moving up to positions of increased responsibility, and you are left behind. This doesn't necessarily mean you are about to be fired, but it should be a signal that your future—at least with that company—is limited and you should begin putting feelers out elsewhere.

Obviously, your own instincts will be the best barometer of whether your job is secure, and I urge you not to jump to conclusions based solely upon the signs I've just mentioned. I do suggest, however, that everyone—particularly in a volatile industry like data processing—be aware of the possibility their job might not last forever and be constantly considering alternatives, should the need to start looking arise. So often, employees view loyalty as a two-way street. They give it their all and assume that the company will play what used to be a paternal role in their lives for so long as they wish to stay. Those days are gone forever. A company will rid itself of people it considers unnecessary to its plans for growth and success. You, the employee, should place *your* growth and success at the center of your thinking. So long as you receive a check, you owe your employer loyalty and your best effort. Other than that, you must view yourself *as a business,* and plan for *its* growth. If you think the ax is about to fall, you may want to preempt it by arranging a meeting with your boss, indicating that you have the feeling that he's not 100 percent satisfied with your performance. Tell your boss that you like the company and the job, if that's true, and ask how you can improve your performance. This might very well work—in any event, it's worth trying.

Dealing with the Ax

Analyzing signals and goals and anticipating being fired is different from suffering the actual act. It's a devastating time for everyone. It represents rejection. It strikes a major blow at your self-confidence. It sets up a series of fears that compound as the ramifications start becoming evident to you. How will you live? Is being fired the sort of blemish on your employment record that will make it almost impossible to find another good job?

The first thing you must do is to force yourself to recognize that the clichés at the beginning of this chapter are, in fact, true. Almost everyone has been fired at one time or another, and in most cases it turned out for the better. It can pertain to you, too, provided that you keep your emotions under control and your wits about you and, instead of falling into a depression and its inevitable paralysis, begin taking immediate action.

First of all, being fired doesn't automatically mean that you will lose your job. It pays to put up a fight in this situation, especially if your replacement hasn't been hired yet. However, to put up an effective fight you must do some soul-searching and be honest about those areas of inadequacy or nonproductivity that have led you to this point.

Has your enthusiasm for the job waned, which, invariably, means a lowering of performance?

Have you become careless about your appearance and grooming?

Have personal problems begun piling up and interfering with your performance on the job? I always like to say that it's better to take your work home with you than to bring your home to work.

When answering these questions about yourself, keep putting yourself in your superior's position and see yourself as your boss sees you. This is no time to be kind to yourself. It is a time to sum up the reasons you have been fired without necessarily having been told what they are.

Now, approach your boss again. Under no circumstances become emotional. Get rid of the tears or anger at home or in the restroom before this meeting. Avoid questioning your superior's judgment. That will get you nowhere. Remember that unless your boss is one of those sadistic individuals who enjoy firing people, his or her emotions are strained, too.

Your best approach is to acknowledge that perhaps you haven't been yourself lately but that you have recognized it and have already taken steps to correct it. Don't make excuses. Don't blame others in the department for some of your work being late or not as carefully prepared as in the past. Point to specific things you have done to correct the situation, and suggest that you be given a month to completely turn it around. Here's where that personal personnel file comes in handy. If you have kept records of your accomplishments over the course of your employment, you will be able to pull out some gems and offer them as examples of what you can do again if given the opportunity.

You mustn't be disappointed if you don't receive that extra month you asked for. The best you can hope for is that your boss will agree to reconsider the firing.

That buys you some time, and time is very much in your favor at this point.

If you have managed to buy time, use it productively. Don't view it as simply an extension of your paychecks and spend half your day on the phone looking for another job. If your boss has reconsidered because you asked, respect the decision and give it your all on the job. That doesn't mean that you shouldn't be *preparing* to look for another position. Go back to the chapter in this book on the job search and start planning. Get your network of contacts in order, and update your résumé. Be ready; but don't jump yet.

The percentages are not in your favor in this situation, but this approach has worked for people I know and might work for you. If it doesn't, and your boss informs you that you will have to leave, then it's time to attempt to make that parting as amicable as possible, no matter what feelings of anger you harbor. There is nothing to be gained—and a great deal to be lost—by telling your boss off and storming out of the office.

Instead, ask for certain courtesies, such as the use of an office and telephone to make looking for another job easier. You should have an idea of company policy toward severance benefits, but by discussing them openly you might be able to improve them. Take subtle advantage of your boss's discomfort and feelings of guilt about firing you, in the hope that a more generous severance offer will be made.

Do everything possible to establish a pleasant, professional relationship with your boss before leaving. The reference that comes out of that will probably be much more in your favor than if you leave under a cloud of rancor and bitterness. In fact, ask whether you can count on your boss for a good reference. The odds are in your favor that you will get what you want.

11

WHEN YOU'RE THE BOSS

Every boss has a boss. At the very top is a boss called the customer.

The higher your position, the more subordinates you'll have, each looking to you for leadership and guidance upon which to help peg their career aspirations.

You'll look back and realize how little time has passed since you sent out your résumés and went through interviews with various levels of management. Now the tables are turned. Now—along with the technical expertise that has gotten you this far (coupled with the other requisites for success mentioned throughout this book)—you must *manage*.

Good DP management is not a seat-of-the-pants exercise. Effective management has been the focus of study for many years, and out of that ongoing analysis has come a massive catalogue of techniques and approaches *that work*.

But, while sound management techniques apply across the board in every area of business, the data-processing field has added some new wrinkles. For instance, as business becomes more dependent upon computers, and the investment of time and money to program grows by leaps and bounds, the demands upon DP management to choreograph systems that will serve the end user is more important than ever before. Incorporating end-user needs with an MIS department requires delicacy, the consummate practice of politics, patience, tolerance of frustration, and, on top of those realities, a keenly honed ability to look ahead and anticipate changing needs. By the time a complicated system is developed and installed to support, for example, a large payroll department, the original stipulated specifications will have changed significantly. If it takes two years to implement such a system—and the two-year rule was a standard not too long ago—the system will be obsolete before it is up and running. This puts a particularly heavy burden on the DP manager, who must find ways to shorten the span between concept and operation.

In line with this, the evaluation of programs available from outside sources now takes up more and more of a DP manager's time. Available computer solutions to business problems are staggering in number. Are the payroll department's needs better served by hiring additional staff programmers, or are outside sources more cost-efficient and, in the long haul, will they better serve the needs of the department and the company? What about educating payroll to the inevitable reality that no system, whether developed in-house or outside, will precisely match every last demand of the department? Add to that the natural human resistance to large-scale change, particularly when it comes to having to learn a new technology, and the magnitude of the DP manager's role becomes obvious. Top management in a company tends to like things the way they were, and the DP manager— probably younger, and perhaps infatuated by the mystique and jargon of computers—comes up with ways to beat down that wall of resistance. This is important because not only must the system be installed and operating, but the people using it have to be positive enough to not sabotage it, through either neglect, lack of interest, or deliberate foot-dragging in accepting it.

It should be evident to you, particularly if you have had the opportunity to see various DP departments in action, that those who successfully manage computer operations have their hands full. So will you, once you reach that point in your career.

Before we discuss effective management techniques, let me again bring up the "Peter Principle." This expression was coined years ago to explain why so many talented people fall on their faces as they climb the success ladder in whatever industry or profession they have chosen to pursue. What happens, according to the principle, is that these people rise to their "level of incompetence." A brilliant and dedicated teacher becomes principal of a school and does a terrible job. Why? Being a good teacher doesn't necessarily translate into being a good administrator, with all its inherent political problems of dealing with school boards and PTAs, and having to manage other teachers. The same holds true for brilliant and dedicated project leaders, senior analysts, or software engineers who are elevated to a top management job that involves skills and interests far beyond the technical ones they are comfortable with. The fact is, there are people who should not be promoted beyond their "level of competence," because they are doomed to failure.

As you forge ahead in your career as a data processor, it would be wise to keep looking into yourself, as I've suggested you do from the very beginning, and try to establish in your own mind *your* level of incompetence. For you, dealing with short-term problem-solving as a project leader might be exactly the niche in which you function best. To accept a promotion to DP manager could plunge you into another whole world in which you're unhappy and, because of this, will not make best use of your talents.

Then again, your personality and interests might make you the perfect candidate for eventual promotion to your company's top data-processing management position, or even eventually to the presidency of the company itself. Take the time to know yourself; your happiness over the course of many years is at stake.

No matter what level of management you reach, you are going to be faced with the difficult task of hiring people to work for you. You might have an excellent personnel department to fall back on, but you will still be the one charged with making the final decision. Recalling one of my studies mentioned earlier, entry-level data processors were hired 68 percent of the time by DP management, while Personnel was involved only 14 percent. When it came to hiring experienced data processors, DP's direct involvement rose to 74 percent, while Personnel did the direct hiring 12 percent of the time. What that means to you, the data-processing manager, is that along with all the computer knowledge you have had to amass up to this point, you are now called upon to become a hiring expert, which leads to the first rule of good management: *you are only as good as the people you hire.*

The term "leveraging" is popular these days as companies perform "leveraged buyouts" of other firms. For you, a data-processing manager, the people working for you can and should be used to leverage your continued reach for success. Your reputation rests upon their performance, and by carefully developing and nurturing a top-notch DP department, your star rises a lot faster. There is, of course, a downside: hire the wrong people and your star will fade in direct proportion to their failure to produce for you.

How to Hire Smart

After more than thirty-five years of being intimately involved in the whole subject of hiring, I distilled what I'd learned into a book published by Crown, entitled *Robert Half on Hiring* (also in paperback by Plume). I mention this to point you toward a readily available source of information on how to hire smart. What's important is that now that you are a boss, much of your future success will depend upon the staff you choose to bring onto your working team. Hiring is not a management function to be handled intuitively. Too much rides on it, including your department's success, your company's success, and your success.

While encouraging you to explore the subject in greater depth, I have included some important, workable ideas that you might keep in mind when going about the difficult process of hiring people.

Finding Good Candidates

• Your personnel department will perform many of the routine duties associated with attracting candidates. It will place want ads in newspapers and trade journals, contact a service specializing in providing experienced people whose qualifications match up with your needs (Robert Half is one), and handle the tedious and difficult task of screening résumés.

However, hiring data-processing personnel is a highly specialized task, and it's my opinion, as well as the opinion of many personnel directors, that interviewing data-processing personnel should be handled by the DP department, and for the higher-level positions, the DP manager must do the interviewing.

If the people doing the initial interviewing do not fully understand data-processing nuances and terminology and the similarity (or lack of similarity) of various hardware and software, they run the risk of eliminating the very people who might perfectly fit the job; they may end up submitting those who seem to conform best to the corporate culture, and whose résumés appear to conform to the job specifications. I believe it works better to have DPers approve of the candidate first, and then send the candidate to the personnel department for reference checking and other hiring procedures.

But you should augment the personnel department's efforts by using your network of contacts within data processing to identify talented people who are out of work or, for various reasons, are looking to change jobs. Your contacts with professional data-processing organizations can be especially helpful.

• Look to yourself, your family, your circle of friends, and the employees already working for you as sources of leads. We've been handed the myth that hiring friends, or friends of friends, is bad practice. That really doesn't make a lot of sense if you think about it. If one of your employees recommends someone who is hired, that person is putting himself or herself on the line and will be careful about whom they recommend to you. Another advantage (and when we get to reference checking it will become more apparent) is that when an employee or friend recommends someone, there comes with that person a built-in reference from someone you know and trust.

Let me clarify one thing, however, about *depending* upon recommendations from friends. One of my studies showed that only 38 percent of friends will give you a candid reference about a former employee of theirs. The moral is to check references thoroughly, no matter who recommends the candidate.

• Another hiring myth we've had imposed on us is that we should never hire people older than we are. Again, that doesn't withstand scrutiny when you consider that older people are often more reliable, loyal, and productive, and, contrary to the myth, do not resent taking orders from younger people.

• Another myth: don't hire people who are "over-qualified" for the job. True, such individuals may become bored and may eventually leave, but if you have made good use of them while they worked for you, you will have gotten your money's worth. Besides, if you treat them properly, they may stay with you, which gives you an "overqualified" person to help in that career leveraging I talked about earlier.

• Still another myth has to do with never hiring people who are related to others in your company. If both are good workers, you will end with a situation in which company loyalty becomes a family affair, which has its advantages.

• Avoid the natural temptation to look only for candidates who have extensive experience in precisely what your department is doing. I'm not suggesting eliminating those people from consideration, but I do recommend placing more emphasis on innate talent, rather than going for recycled "experts." Hiring only from a pool of such people results in inbreeding within your department that is not conducive to innovation and aggressive problem-solving.

• Make sure you understand that your own prejudices must be sidetracked from the hiring process before you interview candidates. I've known top executives who were so consumed with prejudices that by the time they finished informing the personnel department of traits in candidates that would rule them out, they were left with an impossibly narrow field from which to choose. One such gentleman was the president of a small firm who would never hire a fat man because, in his words, "Fat people steal." I know another executive who will hire only people born under certain astrological signs.

Think of all the prejudices you've come across in business, such as the myth that short people all have inferiority complexes and aren't natural leaders, or that redheads have bad tempers. The list of myths that, for too many, have become beliefs is long and depressing. Eyes too close together indicate a shifty personality; a receding chin is a sure sign of a wimp who lacks aggressiveness; a bow tie on a man means that he will never be a team player; bald men who wear a "rug" are covering their hairless domes because they lack self-confidence.

Take all those prejudices, eliminate a candidate because he or she possesses them, and you may see your competitor end up with a bald man wearing a red wig—who has a receding chin, whose eyes are close together, and who is left-handed—leading that other company in burying you competitively.

Prejudices are distasteful in every walk of life. They certainly have no place in the hiring process.

Judging All Those Résumés

Every résumé you've written in your career was conceived to accomplish two things—to maximize strengths and to gloss over weaknesses. You should read résumés from candidates for the job you are trying to fill with the knowledge that they are trying to accomplish the same thing. If a job candidate has taken the proper time and given the proper thought to a résumé, it will do a pretty good job of both. This doesn't constitute dishonesty. Rather, it stems from a realization that it is necessary to sell yourself in a résumé, just as you did. Outright lying on a résumé is another matter. Unfortunately, a lot of people do it, which is why reference checking is such a crucial part of the hiring procedure.

Here are a few quick hints about reading résumés:

• Look for achievements on the résumé, rather than simply a listing of experience and credentials. What the candidate achieved for previous employers might indicate what he or she can achieve for you, and should represent the thing you're most interested in.

• I have often remarked that a résumé is like a balance sheet without liabilities. Also, people tend to put the least flattering material at the bottom of the résumé and their most attractive attributes at the top.

Therefore, read a résumé from the bottom up. You'll be surprised at what insight it can give you into the candidate.

• It isn't often that you will run across a résumé in which the candidate admits to having been fired from a previous job. That's someone to take a closer look at. In the meantime, accept the fact that more than half the people who come to you for a job, and who claim to be presently employed, have a working arrangement with their current employer to terminate at a prescribed date—or they are not working at all (the résumé is old). Add to that the reality that most people who claim to have quit a job were actually fired. But don't consider being fired a pox on the candidate. Remember, almost all of us have been fired at one time or another.

• If the job opening is for an entry-level person, expect that the education section of the résumé will be emphasized. A veteran DPer coming to you for a job will probably downplay education. But keep in mind that it is the education portion of a résumé in which most irregularities occur. Beware of qualifying phrases like "had access to" and "took courses in," because they fudge the issue of whether there has been any real training involved.

• Look for significant gaps in employment, and question them when interviewing the candidate. Again, verifying dates of employment will eventually become an important part of reference checking.

Interviewing

People coming in for a job interview are nervous. You certainly were. Remember? Unfortunately for many qualified job candidates, the tension of the moment is magnified by an inept, unprepared interviewer. Don't be one of those; it isn't fair to the candidate, and ultimately it sabotages your effort to staff your department with the best talent available.

There's a world of successful people who refuse to acknowledge the fact that interviewing involves specific and tangible skills that should be acquired and cultivated. So many executives trust their intuition when interviewing candidates for jobs within their departments, and as a result they pass over the best and end up with much less than the best. If you realize that hiring smart is vital to your future success, you won't approach interviewing in this haphazard manner. Instead, you will avail yourself of good material on the subject of interviewing so that you approach it with a professional, productive attitude.

• First of all, make it a policy to keep accurate records of what occurs during each interview. The reason this is so important is that my studies indicate that the first person interviewed for a job has the worst chance of getting it. Why? We all tend to respond more favorably to our most recent experiences, and the ideal candidate who had the misfortune of being first, second, or third in line may slip through your fingers simply because you have not kept proper notes. Establish a solid rating system so that after seeing a dozen or so candidates, the first—and perhaps the best—isn't lost in the shuffle.

• Pay particular attention during interviews to how much the candidate wants the job. I recommend this because when it comes time to make the final decision, and if there is considerable doubt in your mind between two or three candidates, the one who wanted it most will probably turn out to be your best choice.

• Know what you want to accomplish in an interview before it begins. Have a plan; go over the candidate's résumé and application form so that you don't waste time asking questions about things that are already sitting on the desk in front of you. Make notes about items from the résumé that you want to explore further. Know well in advance the areas you want to cover, so that when the interview is over, you aren't faced with having dwelled too long on some subjects at the expense of getting to those that really interest you.

• Devote whatever time is set aside for the interview *to the interview*. Give the candidate the courtesy of an uninterrupted block of time. (Ninety-five percent of our survey respondents agreed that you should take whatever steps are necessary to avoid interruptions during a job interview.)

• Conduct the interview yourself. While it may be necessary at times to have others from your company involved, it's best to go it alone. Then, if you are impressed by certain candidates, pass them on to others involved in the decision-making process.

• In line with the above, try to narrow down the number of people who will be involved in the ultimate hiring decision. The more people adding their voices to the decision, the more likely you will end up with a "compromise candidate." That translates into *mediocre*.

• Phrase your questions carefully. Don't use closed-ended questions that are calculated to bring forth "yes" and "no" answers. Don't lead candidates by giving them the answers within the question: "What do you like best about data processing, creating new programs?" Throw in a hypothetical question: "How would you react if we assigned you an urgent program that involved long stretches of time without days off?"

I've come to the conclusion that one of the most productive ways of questioning job candidates is to ask them to answer your questions the way they think their references would answer them. Make note of their replies. Then, when you talk to the reference, ask the same question. If the answer differs dramatically, you can mention what the candidate said and discuss reasons why the answers are different.

Tracking Those Elusive References

It's only a coincidence that the acronym LIAR comes out of the good advice "Look Into All References."

Reference checking can be tedious and time-consuming, but it's worth every minute to verify a candidate's background. And if the employee will report directly to you, check the references yourself (at least the most important ones). The fact is, according to studies on the subject, that 30 percent of all job seekers lie on their résumé, not including lies of omission. That a candidate in whom you are interested has stretched the truth a bit doesn't necessarily mean you should rule out that person out for the job, but it does pay for you to know to what extent embellishment has been practiced, and in what areas.

• Also, use the networking approach to check references. References provided by the candidate may not be your best source of information, because the candidate would not have given them to you if he or she weren't confident of a good one. Use those references to build a network of other people with whom you can speak, and follow up every lead.

• If you are filling a really important job and have narrowed down your choice to one or two people, try to check some of the references in person. A face-to-face meeting is always a better way to elicit information. It also allows you to read facial expressions and body language that might say more than words about the person's reaction to the candidate. The next best way is to use the telephone. An ineffective way of going after a reference is by mail. The worst way would be to rely on a reference handed to you by the candidate. People are reluctant in these litigious days to say anything bad about somebody in writing.

• Don't hesitate to use a private investigatory service when important jobs in your department are being filled. Good ones are around. Some services specialize in checking candidates' educational background. Others deal in broader background checks. Obviously it will cost your company some money, but not nearly so much as bringing the wrong person into your organization.

• Don't stop with one or two favorable references. Bear these statistics in mind, which came from a study we conducted on the subject of references: while 72 percent of top management indicated that it was prepared to give a candid reference in person, and a roughly equal number (75 percent) said they expected candid references, only 43 percent of personnel managers indicated that they were prepared to give a candid reference, compared to 65 percent who said they expected candid references. Add these numbers to another of my studies that reveals that even your best friends can't be counted on to give you a candid reference. You can see that there are good reasons for digging long and deep into a candidate's background.

• An applicant should be informed that all references will be checked. A nice way to do this without sounding threatening is to suggest that the candidate check your company's references, too. This puts you on an equal footing and, at the same time, plants a useful suggestion in the candidate's mind. Job candidates should check companies with the same diligence as companies check candidates. (If the applicant is currently employed, an offer can be made subject to a satisfactory reference.)

The entire process of reference checking and its importance to American business has occupied a great deal of my thought over the past several years. One of the results is my booklet, "How to Check References When References Are Hard to Check." It is free and is available to the business public through local Robert Half franchised offices so long as the supply holds out. Malcolm Forbes, whom I quoted earlier in the book, has this to say about the booklet: "In our present suit-happy society, checking references for the real meaning is as difficult an art as writing them. No service booklet could be, to me, more valuable—invaluable is more like it—than Robert Half's 'How to Check References When References Are Hard to Check.' "

I echo Mr. Forbes's feelings about reference checking, and can only urge you, as you grapple with the many difficult aspects of managing, to be sure that reference checking is an important part of your hiring procedure.

Once You Have Made the Choice

Don't waste time bringing the person you have chosen into the company. I've seen it happen countless times: you make your choice, but establish a starting time too far into the future. During that time, a better job is offered the candidate, and you end up being rejected.

And plan for your new employee's first days on the job. It's demoralizing to a new person to hang around doing little because no one has taken the time and interest to prepare. Have projects that the new employee can get into almost immediately.

Do You Really Need a New Employee?

Understaffing or overstaffing a department can have serious budget and productivity consequences. Avoid both by carefully examining the needs of the DP department you now head. A good sign that you're overstaffed is that no one ever works overtime. It's cheaper to pay for occasional overtime than to carry excess help on a permanent basis.

• If someone leaves your department, distribute the work that person had done among other staff members. It's interesting how often the departed employee's work can be handled by others, negating the need to hire a replacement.

• Many highly skilled and experienced data processors are now available through temporary services, such as Accountemps. Avoid permanent overstaffing by bringing in these specialists during peak work loads. Not only will it save you money, but you might find it contributing substantially to your department's efficiency.

• Promote from within whenever possible. It's good for morale. Also, it means you are dealing with known entities. There is no need to check references again on someone who has been working for you for a while and doing a good job.

Handling the Tough Job of Firing Someone

Most employees who are fired expect it. Moreover, most of them admit to themselves that they deserved it.

Having mediocre, nonproductive employees in a department adversely affects everyone. The mediocre employee who keeps the job never advances; good workers become discouraged and look for employment elsewhere; those who stay under these conditions often feel a kinship with the mediocre employee, which means you eventually end up with an entire department of such people.

If the employee who is to be fired reports directly to you, then it's up to you to do the distasteful task yourself. Once you have made up your mind to terminate the employee, do it. Do your best to minimize embarrassment. Be prepared with the payroll check to date plus severance pay and information about details of health plans and insurance. Under no conditions should you lie to the employee.

One word of caution: if you are considering firing someone, make sure it's for cause, and not based on personal considerations that might kick back on you later in the form of a lawsuit. Document every employee's performance on the job, so that when it comes time to break the bad news, you have the ammunition to back it up.

Leverage your career by learning how to hire smart.

12

BECOMING A BETTER MANAGER

The biggest failure of management is not knowing what's going on.

Management is both an art and a science.

The "art" factor comes out of the individual's basic makeup—level of sensitivity to others, attitudes about life and work, innate organizational skills, natural ease of getting along with people, sense of humor, general outlook on life, priorities, built-in value system, and thousands of other factors that define us as individual human beings.

The "science" aspect of management does not come from within. Rather, it is learned over a period of time through a combination of experience, training, and, most important, willingness to acknowledge it as a teachable skill and to strive to learn it.

Unfortunately, many men and women in data processing are, by their own admission, lacking in managerial skills. This finding came out through another of my studies. We first asked top management to evaluate the managerial skills of data-processing managers reporting to them. Sixty-four percent of them felt that their DP managers were weak in those skills. We then asked the DP managers themselves how they would rate their skills as managers, and, believe it or not, 46 percent of them believed their management skills were lacking. In a sense, this can be viewed as a positive finding if those who recognize their inadequacies act upon that knowledge by taking steps to improve their managerial knowledge and techniques. The first step in anyone's improvement is to recognize a weakness. If you feel you are shaky in this area, by all means take whatever steps are necessary to correct the situation.

Going from a lower level—more technical hands-on jobs in data processing—up through the management ranks, in which each plateau carries with it responsibility for more people, demands a set of skills that data-processing training doesn't prepare you for. No longer can you depend upon your computer abilities. You have to call upon a whole new reservoir of knowledge and insight that you'd better fill to the brim to succeed and to reap the resulting rewards. Those in management are faced with problems that are more intangible and all-encompassing than the DPers working under them must deal with, and the approach to solving those problems carries you into a new dimension of business life.

If you have reached a managerial level, it's probably obvious that you now have both an up and a down relationship with others. Until becoming a manager, your primary thrust was upward—developing relationships with those above you. Now, while you continue to do that as you seek even more responsible and loftier positions, you must relate with those below you if you are to succeed. It all comes back to the same thing: *people* are at the heart of all business, including the most highly technical and automated, and it ultimately will be your *people skills*—up and down—that will determine your ultimate career success.

As with every other aspect of the management function, much of what you do will be instinctive, and based upon your own individuality. But in today's complex business climate, you can't depend upon instinct to get through. Instead, your natural abilities have to be supplemented by what you can *learn* about effective management, including the handling of people who report to you.

Time

Managing the productive time of people who work for you is crucial to a department's success. There is only so much time available, and it must be carefully weighed against department and company objectives if they are to be met in a timely fashion. Managers who successfully manage time get more done in *less* time. That's the key to good time management: making maximum use of it.

"Do as I say, not as I do" is sometimes valid where managing people is concerned, but not when it comes to managing time. You, the DP manager, will find it virtually impossible to effectively schedule your staff if you aren't good at planning and keeping to your own schedule. Managing your own time, now that you will have less of it, is something you should work at very hard.

Successful people waste very little time. If they are going to the bank and know they will have to stand in line, they bring with them something that they have been meaning to read, or they use the time to think out a problem that the crush of daily pressure at the office precludes. They make productive use of commuting time by reading on the train or by listening to helpful instructional tapes on their car stereo system. For them, part of planning a business trip is deciding what sort of work to carry on the plane that can readily by done in-flight.

Successful people value their time enough to *find* the time to improve their reading skills and speed. They learn to skim voluminous reports in order to quickly sum up the essence of them. They also recognize that good physical condition contributes to effective use of time. It promotes more restful sleep and boosts energy levels after long hours at a project, with the promise of more to come.

I've made it a point for years to always have a mini tape recorder with me. I like to start my day early in the morning with a long walk, and I find this to be a particularly fertile time for me to think out problems that I know I'll be facing that day. Such thoughts are fleeting, however, which is why the tape recorder has become an indispensable item in my pocket.

A good area in which managing time pays off involves business meetings. As you progressed through the data-processing ranks, how many managers have you worked for who call a meeting and then spend an incredible amount of valuable time getting it started? Meetings should be carefully thought out and planned, and a tight agenda should be adhered to. The same holds true for conferences with individual employees. Know what you want to accomplish when you call someone into your office, and stick to the subject.

Establish with your employees an understanding that you don't enjoy wasting time and you expect them to respect that. By doing this, you will find yourself having more available time during your workday and, simultaneously, will help establish in your employees the same attitude toward their own workday.

Successful executives put considerable planning into their office decor and surroundings to discourage irrelevant conversations. They keep distracting objects to a minimum, which cuts down on idle chitchat about them. They establish, in a friendly way, an atmosphere in which it is expected that visitors will get their points across quickly, without unnecessary deviation.

You, the DP manager, have to set the tone when it comes to making productive use of a department's time. You can't hang out by the water cooler or copying machine and expect your employees to avoid that indulgence.

Communicating with Your Staff

It should be safe to assume that because you have risen to a managerial position in data processing, you have developed a workable set of communication skills, verbal and written. They undoubtedly have been important and have enabled you to transmit your knowledge and ideas to higher-ups, who, in turn, responded by promoting you, or by hiring you for a higher position than you'd previously held.

But now, not only must you continue to do that with your superiors, but you must communicate effectively with those who report to you. In many ways, that can be more difficult.

As I've noted throughout this book, poor communication is at the heart of countless failures in business life. You have undoubtedly worked for a supervisor who had poor communication skills and whose instructions were often vague and contradictory, making it difficult for you and your co-workers to get the job done. That's a situation you want to avoid with your employees. Many supervisors seem to go through their days assuming that an entire department can read their mind, and they become upset when a job isn't done to their specifications, never recognizing and admitting that they did a terrible job of explaining what they wanted.

Become comfortable with the written word. Putting instructions in writing is preferable to giving verbal instructions, for two reasons. First, the employee has the paper to refer to, instead of trying to remember what you said. Second, it establishes a written record of what you wanted done, something you can turn to in the event that it isn't accomplished and there is a claim on the part of an employee that "You didn't tell me that."

Of course, there is always a certain risk in putting

things in writing. If you're not sure what it is you want—and your memo reflects it—the document can end up being used against you by your own boss, who may be unhappy with your department's failure. But to avoid written communication for that reason represents the sort of defensive management that everyone finds offensive. Think out what you wish to convey to an employee, and write it down with clarity and conciseness. Don't churn out memos without taking the time to read them over before they reach their destination. Professional writers often say, "All good writing is rewriting." Put your thoughts down on paper quickly, but then scrutinize the way you expressed them. Spell things out. Be clear. Don't be a lazy writer. Recognize that a set of clear instructions saves time down the line, because the project gets done right the first time.

Keep written communications short and to the point. Just as you wish to avoid verbal rambling in a meeting, you don't want to bore people with long, pointless memos that could have said the same thing in a paragraph or two. Take the space to get your point across, but don't pad or reach for complicated words when simple ones will do.

Just as good writing is basically an exercise in clear thinking, so is verbal presentation. Before calling in one of your staff to complain about a project, or to give instructions about a new one, take a few minutes to think it out, particularly how you wish to express your thoughts to the individual.

Learn how to best apply the "good news—bad news" approach to criticism. If a good employee has done something wrong, set a less-severe tone by beginning the conversation with an anecdote about when you fouled up at some point in your career. This attitude goes hand-in-hand with a general management philosophy of bossing by motivation, not fear.

Praise good work as often as possible, rather than communicating only displeasure at failed projects. If you have to penalize an employee for something, try to make the penalty less severe than the employee expected.

Look for compromise; always try to correct a situation rather than complain about it.

It's always amazing to me how, in this world of imperfect people (which includes every one of us), a large percentage of imperfect people look to hire perfect people and to have their departments staffed by nothing but perfect people. Accept the imperfect nature of our world, celebrate it, smile often at its foibles, and strive to be a manager who motivates and inspires those around you, whose performance will reflect on none other than . . . you.

Three final thoughts:

If you have trouble smiling, try this little technique. When you want to smile, think of the word "smile." Your face will reflect the thought, just as if you think of the word "grouch," it will mirror that, too.

Be committed to developing in yourself one of the most important traits in every successful manager and executive I've ever known, and that is reflecting on the glory of the people who work for you. If a project has gone especially well, heap praise on your people. Don't reserve it for yourself. Top management respects people who function this way, and who have hired the right people, trained them, and been able to nurture and keep them. Conversely, don't blame your staff when a project fails. "The buck stops here" should be your operative philosophy.

Finally, on the general subject of communication, *learn to listen*. Encourage ideas from your staff, and really think about them; don't simply make it an exercise to give your employees the impression that they have influence on you and the department. Along the same lines, if you decide to institute a suggestion box, don't turn it into a coffin by burying what's in it. If you are going to encourage suggestions, at least read them all and consider them carefully.

Good ideas for managing people have been developed over many years, and they are available to you in books, tapes, and magazine articles, if you take the time and effort to explore them. The results can be spectacular.

13

SELF-EMPLOYMENT

*Those who are entrepreneurially inclined
work long hours, take big risks, have
maximum stress, and love every
minute of it.*

On Your Own

There are two reasons we leave jobs—because we
choose to or because we're fired.

In most cases (assuming you weren't fired), you will
leave one job to go to another, presumably one that
offers greater challenge, financial rewards, growth opportunity, and whatever else you respond to. But an
increasing number of people are leaving jobs these days
to go into their own businesses, especially in the
data-processing field.

The topsy-turvy growth of the computer age has
caused immense confusion in corporations across
America and, indeed, around the world. Old-fashioned
methods of running a business have gone by the board,
and old-fashioned managers are feeling the effects of
this. Computers play a vital role in many businesses,
dominate others, and, according to all the best available

research, will be at the heart of every business by 1995. This has created a fertile field in which the bright and energetic with a firm knowledge of data processing can leave the corporate structure and forge lucrative, exciting business ventures of their own—with their former corporations often becoming needy and generous customers.

While the chaotic nature of data processing has played a significant role in the proliferation of people from its ranks going out on their own, the *personality* of many DPers has also contributed to the movement. Those studies I cited in the beginning of the book about the general personality profile of a data processor include such words as "maverick," "loner," "individual," "dogmatic," "free spirit." Those of you who truly can be described by one or several of these words may have been having trouble functioning smoothly within a large, bureaucratic, corporate society, and are ripe for a move to a business of your own in which those stifling factors aren't present.

Add to those first two ingredients the fact that entrepreneurship has been at the heart of America's business and industrial growth since the earliest days of its existence. I'm confident that there isn't a man or woman working in this society who has not, at least once, given some serious thought to starting a business.

Should the combination of the above factors act as a signal for all data processors to strike out on their own?

Absolutely not.

What these factors *do* indicate is that if you are the

sort of person who not only has the computer knowledge necessary for a successful business of your own in
the field, but also possesses the myriad other factors
necessary for *anyone*—in *any* business—to make a go
of it, it might be for you.

Here are some things you should consider before
making a decision to leave a secure corporate job to test
the entrepreneurial waters.

First, let's see whether you fall into a general background that seems to characterize most successful
entrepreneurs. A recent Gallup study uncovered the
following:

• Fifty-nine percent of successful entrepreneurs in
the survey were in the upper sixth of their class, and 38
percent were average or below average.

• One in six was suspended from school, and a third
of them were fired at least once in their careers before
striking out on their own. (We believe *most* people
were fired at one time or another, but are too embarrassed to admit it—even to a survey interviewer.)

• Most belonged to few organizations, substantiating
the basic personality profile of the "loner."

• Thirty-eight percent of them named their father as
the most influential person in their lives.

• Almost half of them did not fall into the typical
white Anglo-Saxon ethnic background. They emerged
from a broad spectrum of nationalities.

- Most came from middle-class families. Twenty-seven percent of them said their father had never finished high school.

- They did not, for the most part, come out of rich, privileged backgrounds. They were not necessarily deprived in childhood, but their families had to struggle to make ends meet.

An interesting pattern emerges from the Gallup study: successful entrepreneurs generally don't battle their way out of the ghetto, any more than they use family money to start their own business. There is, however, a strong influence of a family that perhaps has enough money to nurture a child but certainly not to indulge it. In other words, there has been a flame built beneath these people to do better, and the study goes on to identify such personal attributes as tenacity, stubbornness, no fear of failure, and a determination to beat the odds. Eight out of ten new businesses fail in America, but that pessimistic statistic doesn't deter entrepreneurs. They don't think about the eight failures, only envision themselves in that 20 percent success category.

If you don't meet the profile of the Gallup study, does it mean you should abandon dreams of starting your own business? Of course not. What has represented the successful entrepreneur in the past has no bearing on what future entrepreneurs will be made of. What is more significant, however, are the rules for success, which really haven't changed very much, and probably won't, at least in the near future.

Learn Before You Teach

I recently was served in a restaurant by a delightful young man who, through the course of our conversation, indicated that he was working toward completion of his undergraduate degree in computer sciences at a local university. I asked him what sort of job he intended to go after once he graduated.

"I want to work for myself. I have some people who'll back me" was his reply.

I pointed out to him that he might be better served working for other people for a while before thinking of branching out on his own. "There's a lot to learn," I said, "and the best way to learn it is to be working for people who've been through it and who can pass on valuable information to you."

Whether my comment had any impact on him is doubtful, but I hope it has on you. In what has often been called the "Me Generation," instant gratification has come to be expected by many young people. Solid apprenticeships are avoided by those wanting full status too soon in their lives. The spate of insider-trading scandals on Wall Street points to bright, talented, and educated young people wanting too much too soon. We seem to have become a nation of people expecting instant success, instant wealth, instant recognition, and, most sadly, instant happiness, which, in reality, comes only from having achieved those previous things through hard work and dedication to a goal.

Perhaps that unfortunate truth is at the heart of the eight failures out of ten attempts to start one's own business. We hear a lot about small businesses failing because of inadequate start-up capital to sustain the business through its initial lean times. It might be more appropriate to question the sufficiency of knowledge, training, and experience on the part of those who leaped too soon at the American dream and who did not have the *inner* resources to sustain themselves through those lean times.

What underlies the failure of so many new businesses is the belief on the part of individuals starting them that knowledge of the subject or product being offered is sufficient for success. Certainly, there are millions of you in data processing who know your stuff when it comes to hardware and software. But unless you have been exposed to the business world and have come to learn and understand it beyond the confines of your role as a data processor, your chances of succeeding are low when you open the doors to a business that bears your name.

Opportunities for DP Entrepreneurs

The best opportunities for you to become self-employed will stem from identifying a need that isn't being met. That's the key to all success—giving people something they need and don't have. Here are some obvious areas you might explore.

1. Teaching the PC (personal computer) to others. This can be done in your spare time, which gives

you an opportunity to determine whether it will support a full-time effort and, at the same time, put extra money in the bank to be used as start-up capital for your own business. This approach goes hand-in-hand with my previous suggestion that you moonlight outside your regular job. Besides providing extra money, enabling you to build your network of contacts within the community and industry, and giving you additional knowledge, it also can be the precursor (no pun intended) to a business of your own. One of the advantages of moonlighting is that it can, over a long period of time, *naturally* develop into a full-time business. That's been the case with many people, and it could be for you. The thing to watch out for is that you don't rush from part time into full time. Just as there is the appropriate moment to go after a bigger and better job within data processing, there is the right time to make the entrepreneur's move. Don't be impetuous; it seldom pays off.

2. Using temporary work to get your feet wet. Often, DPers who yearn to start their own business operate from a deficit in that their experience has been confined to a narrow scope. Taking temporary jobs through a specialized service can expose you to a wide variety of data-processing situations.

3. Consulting. I differentiate working temporary jobs and moonlighting from *consulting*, in that it represents a different level of providing outside help

to individuals and companies. Again, it could start as a part-time endeavor, except that your accessibility and availability will be limited by the demands of your permanent job. Still, there are opportunities for part-time consultants in which access to you is not as important as time spent on solving a problem that can be reported in writing.

The term "consultant" can be misleading because it's so often abused and misused. The old line goes that if you're an executive who's out of work, you're a consultant. Lots of people bill themselves as consultants but don't do any consulting. The word has a nice ring to it and is shrouded in enough mystery to preclude questioning. Consultants to industry possess that "out-of-town" magic—anyone being brought in from the outside is expected to know more than those within the company—and this has always rankled permanent employees, who in many cases have been suggesting projects and programs that are ignored until the consultant arrives with the same suggestions, which are enthusiastically embraced as remarkable breakthroughs.

Still, legitimate consultants play a vital role in industry, and the good ones—coming into an ongoing situation without the prejudices of having been inside—apply their third-party and detached view, which often results in fresh vision and new ways of attacking old problems.

There's another saying about consultants, and that is

that gray at the temples is worth another $10,000 a year. Consultants are expected to have wisdom and experience above and beyond those for whom they are consulting. If you are relatively young and inexperienced, the consulting label probably won't work for you. Then again, you may be twenty years old and have developed an approach to a systems or software problem that stands everybody on their ear. If that's the case, however, you are probably better off marketing it across the broad range of business rather than selling your knowledge to one or two clients.

Data-Processing Security

As the use of computers grows to process information on virtually every one of our activities, the problem of computer crime grows at a parallel rate. There are no reliable figures available on how much money is lost each year through computer crime, but one figure, if even close to being accurate, indicates how serious it could be in certain industries. It's estimated that the *potential* loss to Electronic Funds Transfers (EFT) alone is over $30 billion *a day*.

There has been a great deal in the media about computer "hackers," those who tap into corporate and government systems as a lark. Theft is not the intention of the hacker, but the disruption to corporate record-keeping is immense. More important, the ease with which computer hackers have gained access to corporate computer systems has vividly demonstrated to everyone concerned the vulnerability of computer-based corporate and government activities. In that sense, the hackers have done the computer industry a service by creating this awareness.

Perhaps an even greater potential threat to computer confidentiality comes from dishonest and disloyal data processors within companies who use their knowledge and access for their own gain. How easy to add a couple of family names to a computer list of those to receive monthly dividend checks, or to sell vital corporate information to competitors. Blackmail is not unknown, either. There are a number of documented cases in which someone from a data-processing department walked away with important records and offered to sell the information back to the company for a hefty fee.

As a result of all this, every business and government agency that depends upon computers not only must devote considerable attention to developing and running systems, but also must turn an increasing amount of attention and funds to securing those systems.

A business having between 150 and 250 DPers, if properly staffed, can spend $250 million a year or more for security professionals' salaries alone. Many companies, however, have not reached that point in staffing solely to secure systems, which opens up a whole new field for computer-security consultants. Those with intimate knowledge of computer systems are exactly the people to whom industry will turn for solutions to the computer-crime program.

In addition to devising security systems, there is also a need for procedures to be developed to screen out data processors whose ethical background is not what it should be, and to devise ways to supervise DP staffs to insure adherence to security procedures, also formulated by professionals.

As I've pointed out, successful entrepreneurs are the ones who see a need and fulfill it, and computer security represents one kind of opportunity.

Contract Programming

There is a trend in *all* industry to look increasingly to outside services to provide personnel to handle peak loads. The reason for this is obvious: maintaining a large permanent staff means higher overhead, even when the need for workers slacks off during quiet periods. Rather than overstaffing, companies bring in specialists to augment the regular staff, which is cost-efficient. The cost to a company of providing benefits to permanent employees is high; more important, hiring and termination are very expensive and can cause a good company to earn a poor personnel reputation. This is why specialized temporary services and contract programmers flourish.

Because good programmers are in such demand, companies basically have three options when a rash of new programs are suddenly needed. One is to hire from the outside on a temporary, contract basis. The second is to overstaff, bite the bullet when it comes to the overhead, and know that you have enough people on hand for the crunch. The third is to hire or train generalists who can shift from function to function, depending upon the needs of the moment.

What it all comes down to is that there is an excellent market for free-lance programmers to come in and reinforce permanent staff when needed. This can be a good opportunity for you, but there are problems to be considered.

First, the liability-insurance dilemma that is hitting many industries hard would have to be considered from your point of view as an independent programmer. Come in from the outside as an "expert," develop a program for a company that doesn't work and causes that firm to lose money, and you might be on the receiving end of a hefty lawsuit. The same holds true if you are functioning as an independent expert on computer crime and security and the files are stolen. In fact, for anyone starting a business, insurance must be one of the first things considered, and in many cases the cost proves prohibitive, and the insurance is hard to get at any price.

Another problem stems from how the government, particularly the IRS, defines a *contract* programmer. Currently, that definition is being pondered, questioned, and rewritten in Washington in an attempt to clarify when a person truly provides free-lance services and when that person should be considered an employee of the company to which he or she provides the service. There is a long list of criteria that must be met for a company to avoid having to consider an outsider free-lancer part of the permanent staff, and it's harder to justify where a programmer is involved. So much programming must take place on the company's premises, and programming projects put the free-lancer on the job for protracted periods of time. Obviously, a company loses some of the benefit it is seeking if you, a contract programmer, must be considered permanent staff. If you decide to strike out on your own as a contract programmer, become familiar with the legalities. Check with a lawyer so that you can intelligently discuss the problems with a potential customer.

Despite these problems and others, we see more and more talented programmers going out on their own, and if you feel it's for you, there is plenty of opportunity for you to succeed.

Starting a Business

The reason I fervently recommend that you get some solid business experience under your belt by working for others before setting out on your own is that running a business—*any* business—involves dozens of factors that aren't part of your training and experience as a data processor. Obtaining financing is a specialty unto itself, and the terms of whatever financial backing you receive to start your business could make the difference between success and failure.

Then too, there is the need for expert accounting and legal advice if the increasingly complicated laws of our land are to be dealt with effectively.

Marketing your service or product is perhaps the biggest problem. To be done properly, marketing will demand as much or even more of your time than the actual business you have gone into.

Starting your own business is not to be taken lightly. One way to enjoy many of the rewards of running your own show without most of the inherent risks is to work for a large company that fosters the entrepreneurial spirit. The number of such companies is growing as top management recognizes how many valuable products, services, and ideas can come out of a small, independent unit within the larger structure, particularly in high-tech areas. In these situations, bright men and women are, in effect, given their own mini-company to run, with the backing of the corporation. Naturally, the monetary rewards generated by the small unit's success belong to the corporation, not to the individuals, but all the psychic rewards are there—freedom from bureaucratic restrictions (though never total freedom, of course); determining day-to-day work schedules; functioning with a small, compatible staff; satisfaction at pursuing a smaller personal project rather than being involved in much larger, more diffuse corporate pursuits.

The popular term for entrepreneurs functioning within large corporations is "intrapreneur."

One of my favorite stories about intrapreneurs came out of the 3-M Company, where an individual was given his own staff and the resources to develop a super glue. He and his staff failed. The glue they were developing barely stuck at all.

But, having the classic entrepreneurial mentality, this bright fellow saw a whole new market for glue that didn't stick very well, and the very successful Post-It line of note pads was born.

If becoming an intrapreneur won't satisfy your urge

to function on your own, or your company doesn't encourage it, you will have to consider the riskier step of starting your own business. The number of data processors who leave corporate jobs to go into business will undoubtedly grow as the management pipelines become increasingly clogged. DPers are impatient; they respond to growth and challenge, and to opportunities to advance in their careers. Stymied because of the field's having attracted so many talented, creative, and bright men and women, those who find their upward business mobility hindered will look elsewhere—to themselves and to their own initiative outside the corporate structure. Because a number of them will become successful, they will create small businesses that will attract others from larger, more established data-processing jobs who seek the same freedom and opportunity to develop and implement their own ideas. That's a common trait of entrepreneurs, attracting small teams of young people who believe in the idea behind the entrepreneur, and who are willing to risk the security and comfort of a job in order to achieve faster growth and success.

14

JUST THE BEGINNING

Successful people are never satisfied.

Success!

It's such an elusive, arguable term, and it has captured the attention of every American since we became an industrialized society. It carries with it enough definitions and viewpoints to create its own dictionary.

Success in data processing is no different. What you judge to be success in your life will determine the level of aspiration and energy you put into achieving it. It might be satisfied by a lower-level, routine, and hands-on application of a narrow DP skill. It might be keyed to where you work or live, or to the number of vacation days you are given, the level of air conditioning and general surroundings of the workplace, or hundreds of other factors that represent your individual needs.

I've tried in this book to offer advice on making it big in data processing at virtually every level. Where you choose to stop is, again, an expression of your individuality and personal needs. "Making it big in data processing" is in the eye of the beholder—your eye.

Those of you who have not only set your sights on the highest positions in data processing and its management, but hope to leap beyond them into the highest echelons of top management, are entertaining those dreams at a vital point in the history of data processing.

It wasn't long ago that the field was narrow enough in its general contribution to a company's success that the chances of making such a dramatic move were certainly less than probable, and barely possible. In the past, men and women reached the top by coming up through such corporate departments as marketing, sales, finance, and others that were perceived as having direct influence on the company's success and future. Now, with computers moving to the heart of American industry—and with that trend destined to continue in coming years—the importance of your occupation is significant enough to make quantum leaps to the boardroom not only possible, but in some cases, even probable.

What will it take for you to achieve it?

Wanting it.

Preparing for it.

Going after it.

I hope this book will help you to achieve a greater level of success by realizing and understanding that there is much more to success than just technical knowledge. It involves every aspect of the human condition, every facet of us as men and women, no matter what occupation or profession we choose to pursue or what our ultimate goals are.

Data processing—is an established and accepted part of the American business and industrial future. That future is bright.

So is yours.

It's just the beginning.

I wish you well.

APPENDIX

The following pages contain highlights of a study I conceived and developed to help data processors get ahead in their chosen career. It consisted of a 10 percent sampling of data-processing managers and top management of the one thousand largest corporations in the United States. The study was implemented for me by Burke Marketing Research.

Appendix: *Contents*

TABLES

TABLE 1

PERSON RESPONSIBLE FOR HIRING OF DATA-PROCESSING PERSONNEL

	DP MANAGE-MENT %
ENTRY LEVEL	
DP Management	68
Top Management	—
Personnel Management	14
Other	14
Don't Know	4
EXPERIENCED	
DP Management	74
Top Management	2
Personnel Management	12
Other	8
Don't Know	4
SUPERVISORY	
DP Management	54
Top Management	10
Personnel Management	16
Other	12
Don't Know	8

TABLE 2

ATTRIBUTES CONSIDERED TO BE IMPORTANT WHEN HIRING A DATA PROCESSOR

	DP MANAGE-MENT %
Prior Experience	62
Technical Know-how	58
Education	32
Personality	22
Job Stability	20
Appearance	8
Other	6
Don't Know	–

TABLE 3

HIRING SOURCES FOR DP PROFESSIONALS

	DP MANAGE-MENT %
Placing Ads	78
Recruiters & Agencies	76
In-house Recommendations	66
Some Other Way	20
Don't Know	–

TABLE 4

HIRING SOURCES USED MOST OFTEN FOR FINDING DP PROFESSIONALS

	DP MANAGE-MENT %
Recruiters & Agencies	40
Placing Ads	30
In-house Recommendations	12
Some Other Way	8
Don't Know	10

TABLE 5

FREQUENCY OF TEMPORARY-HELP USAGE IN DATA PROCESSING

	DP MANAGE- MENT %
Frequently	22
Sometimes	18
Rarely	42
Never	16
Don't Know	2

TABLE 6

FREQUENCY OF EMPLOYMENT OF ENTRY-LEVEL DATA PROCESSORS

	DP MANAGE- MENT %
Frequently	34
Sometimes	32
Rarely	24
Never	6
Don't Know	4

TABLE 7

MOST IMPORTANT TRAITS OR ATTRIBUTES OF A GOOD DATA PROCESSOR

	TOTAL %	DP MANAGE- MENT %	TOP MANAGE- MENT %
WORKING HABITS (NET)	15	22	8
Good Working Habits	4	8	—
Hard Worker	4	8	—
Accurate	4	4	4
Efficient/Organized	3	2	4
BACKGROUND (NET)	11	12	10
Education	4	8	—
Business Perspective/ Understand Clients' Needs	4	—	8
Experience	3	4	2
All Other Miscellaneous Mentions	2	—	4
Don't Know/No Answer	8	6	10
PERSONAL ATTRIBUTES (NET)	52	62	42
Logical	23	22	24
Ability to Interact/Get Along with People	15	22	8
Communication Skills	8	14	2

	TOTAL %	DP MANAGE- MENT %	TOP MANAGE- MENT %
Open-minded/ Receptive/Willing to Learn/Change	5	8	2
Creative/Good Imagination	4	6	2
Patient	4	4	4
Personality	3	4	2
SKILLS/ABILITIES (NET)	46	44	48
Technical Expertise	16	24	8
Problem-Solving Abilities	10	8	12
Well Trained/Knowl- edgeable About Equipment/How to Use Equipment	9	4	14
Intellectual Ability	9	8	10
Math Skills	5	4	6
Management Skills/ Project Control/Project Planning	3	2	4

TABLE 8

SHOULD A DATA PROCESSOR WITH THREE YEARS OF EXPERIENCE BE LICENSED?

	TOTAL %	DP MANAGE- MENT %	TOP MANAGE- MENT %
Yes	12	14	10
No	75	76	74
Don't Know	13	10	16

TABLE 9

MOST IMPORTANT REASONS FOR THE FAILURE OF SOME DATA PROCESSORS TO GET AHEAD

	TOTAL %	DP MANAGE- MENT %	TOP MANAGE- MENT %
LACK OF MOTIVATION (NET)	29	40	18
Lack of Motivation/ Drive	12	14	10
Lack of Initiative	9	16	2
No Ambition to Get Ahead	6	10	2
Don't Work Hard/Hard Enough	3	2	4

	TOTAL %	DP MANAGE- MENT %	TOP MANAGE- MENT %
All Other Lack of Motivation Mentions	1	2	—
PERSONAL (NET)	26	22	30
Inability to Relate with/Work with People/ Hard to Get Along With	15	16	14
Inability to Communi- cate/Express Self Clearly	6	4	8
Lack of Personality	3	4	2
Not a Good Listener	1	—	2
All Other Personal Mentions	2	—	4
INABILITY TO DO JOB (NET)	7	10	4
Inability to Solve Problems	3	4	2
Inability to Manage	3	6	—
Incompetent/Not Capable of Ability	1	—	2

	TOTAL %	DP MANAGE-MENT %	TOP MANAGE-MENT %
MISCELLANEOUS			
Not Stay Up-to-date/Not Keep Up with Current Technology	10	14	6
Don't Enjoy Work/ Boring Job	2	2	2
Working for Money Only/Not "Into" the Job	2	4	—
All Other Miscellaneous Mentions	9	6	12
Don't Know/No Answer	7	2	12
LACK OF UNDERSTANDING (NET)	17	14	20
Not Understanding Big Picture/Not Relating Tasks to Big Picture	8	6	10
Not Understanding Business Administration/How Business Is Run	4	4	4
Not Understanding Companies' Objectives	3	2	4

	TOTAL %	DP MANAGE-MENT %	TOP MANAGE-MENT %
All Other Lack-of-Understanding Mentions	2	2	2
UNDERQUALIFIED (NET)	12	10	14
Inexperienced	4	4	4
Lack of Technical Skills/Expertise	3	—	6
Lack of Adequate Education	3	4	2
Chose Wrong Career	2	4	—
Not Qualified for Job	1	—	2

TABLE 10

SKILLS OR QUALITIES MISSING IN COLLEGE GRADUATES

	DP MANAGE-MENT %
BUSINESS/EDUCATION (NET)	58
Business Experience/ Practical Experience	44

	DP MANAGE-MENT %
Difference Between Textbooks and Reality	12
Business Education	2
SKILLS (NET)	36
Business Skills	20
Technical Skills	16
Analytic Ability	8
PERSONALITY (NET)	10
Ability to Interact with People	8
Temperament	2
Don't Know/No Answer	8

TABLE 11

PERCENTAGE OF DP EMPLOYEE ABSENTEEISM BY DAY OF WEEK

	DP MANAGE-MENT %
MONDAY	
0 Percent	40
1–4 Percent	26
5–9 Percent	2
30–39 Percent	2
Don't Know	30
TUESDAY	
0 Percent	44
1–4 Percent	18
5–9 Percent	4
30–39 Percent	2
Don't Know	32
WEDNESDAY	
0 Percent	38
1–4 Percent	20
5–9 Percent	6
10–19 Percent	2
Don't Know	34

	DP MANAGE-MENT %
THURSDAY	
0 Percent	42
1–4 Percent	18
5–9 Percent	6
Don't Know	34
FRIDAY	
0 Percent	40
1–4 Percent	16
5–9 Percent	6
20–29 Percent	4
30–39 Percent	4
Don't Know	30

TABLE 12

PERSON TO WHOM HEAD OF DATA PROCESSING REPORTS

	TOTAL %	DP MANAGE- MENT %	TOP MANAGE- MENT %
Vice-President of Finance	14	2	26
Chief Financial Officer	12	16	8
Executive Vice-President	8	2	14
Chief Executive Officer	7	8	6
Corporate Controller	7	8	6.
President	5	—	10
Vice-President of Administration	3	—	6
Group Vice-President	3	—	6
Other Vice-President	1	2	—
Other	34	56	12
Don't Know	6	6	6

TABLE 13

RANKING OF THE HEAD OF DATA PROCESSING COMPARED TO CHIEF FINANCIAL OFFICER AND CORPORATE CONTROLLER

	TOTAL %	DP MANAGE-MENT %	TOP MANAGE-MENT %
CHIEF FINANCIAL OFFICER			
Higher	1	—	2
Lower	86	88	84
Same	12	12	12
Don't Know	1	—	2
CORPORATE CONTROLLER			
Higher	6	4	8
Lower	53	64	42
Same	39	30	48
Don't Know	2	2	2

TABLE 14

LIKELIHOOD OF THE HEAD OF DATA PROCESSING BECOMING THE CHIEF EXECUTIVE OFFICER IN NEXT 10 YEARS

	TOTAL %	DP MANAGE-MENT %	TOP MANAGE-MENT %
Very Likely	2	4	—
Somewhat Likely	5	4	6
Neither Likely nor Unlikely	7	10	4
Somewhat Unlikely	23	20	26
Very Unlikely	62	60	64
Don't Know	1	2	—

TABLE 15

ATTRIBUTES OF DATA-PROCESSING PERSONNEL

	DP MANAGE- MENT %
EVERYTHING ELSE BEING EQUAL, A DATA PROCESSOR WITH A DEGREE IN A RELATED FIELD IS MORE LIKELY TO GET AHEAD THAN ONE WITHOUT A DEGREE	
Agree Strongly	64
Agree Somewhat	26
Neither Agree nor Disagree	—
Disagree Somewhat	2
Disagree Strongly	8
IF YOU HAD TO DO IT ALL OVER AGAIN, YOU WOULD CHOOSE DATA PROCESSING AS YOUR PROFESSION	
Agree Strongly	58
Agree Somewhat	22
Neither Agree nor Disagree	4
Disagree Somewhat	4

	DP MANAGE-MENT %
Disagree Strongly	6
Don't Know	6

DATA-PROCESSING SCHOOLS, IN GENERAL, ARE DOING A GOOD JOB IN EDUCATING COMPUTER PROFESSIONALS

	DP MANAGE-MENT %
Agree Strongly	6
Agree Somewhat	46
Neither Agree nor Disagree	18
Disagree Somewhat	18
Disagree Strongly	8
Don't Know	4

TURNOVER OF DATA-PROCESSING PEOPLE IS SOMEWHAT HEAVIER THAN FOR PERSONNEL IN OTHER DIVISIONS OF THE COMPANY

	DP MANAGE-MENT %
Agree Strongly	32
Agree Somewhat	26
Neither Agree nor Disagree	12
Disagree Somewhat	20
Disagree Strongly	10

	TOTAL %	DP MANAGE- MENT %	TOP MANAGE- MENT %
THE OPPORTUNITIES IN TO-DAY'S BUSINESS CLIMATE ARE BETTER THAN EVER FOR DATA PROCESSORS			
Agree Strongly	72	80	64
Agree Somewhat	22	18	26
Neither Agree nor Disagree	—	—	—
Disagree Somewhat	2	2	2
Disagree Strongly	—	—	—
Don't Know/Not Asked Question	4	—	8
DATA PROCESSING IS AN EXCELLENT FIELD FOR MEN WHO ARE LOOKING TO ADVANCE QUICKLY			
Agree Strongly	32	30	34
Agree Somewhat	34	32	36
Neither Agree nor Disagree	17	22	12
Disagree Somewhat	14	16	12
Disagree Strongly	3	—	6

	TOTAL %	DP MANAGE- MENT %	TOP MANAGE- MENT %
DATA PROCESSING IS AN EXCELLENT FIELD FOR WOMEN WHO ARE LOOKING TO ADVANCE QUICKLY			
Agree Strongly	38	28	48
Agree Somewhat	39	46	32
Neither Agree nor Disagree	10	12	8
Disagree Somewhat	11	12	10
Disagree Strongly	2	2	2
DATA PROCESSORS ARE OFTEN UNDERVALUED AND UNDERPAID			
Agree Strongly	7	10	4
Agree Somewhat	24	26	22
Neither Agree nor Disagree	17	14	20
Disagree Somewhat	33	38	28
Disagree Strongly	15	12	18
Don't Know/Not Asked Question	4	—	8

	TOTAL %	DP MANAGE-MENT %	TOP MANAGE-MENT %
DATA PROCESSORS WHO COMMUNICATE AND ARTICULATE WELL FIND IT A LOT EASIER TO GET AHEAD			
Agree Strongly	74	82	66
Agree Somewhat	22	14	30
Neither Agree nor Disagree	3	2	4
Disagree Somewhat	1	2	—
Disagree Strongly	—	—	—

TABLE 16

MAIN REASON FOR LOSS OF GOOD DP PERSONNEL

	DP MANAGE- MENT %
Lack of Advancement	32
Compensation	30
Other Job Opportunities	12
Challenges Elsewhere	12
Changing Environment	8
Location	6
Bad Management/Lack of Planning	6
Competition	4
All Others	6
Don't Know/No Answer	4

TABLE 17

IS THE DATA-PROCESSING DEPARTMENT CONFUSING?

	TOP MANAGE-MENT %
Yes	40
No	58
Don't Know	2

TABLE 18

SHOULD TOP MANAGEMENT HAVE A WORKING KNOWLEDGE OF DATA-PROCESSING PROCEDURES?

	TOTAL %	DP MANAGE-MENT %	TOP MANAGE-MENT %
Yes	68	60	76
No	29	36	22
Don't Know	3	4	2

TABLE 19

COMPLAINTS ABOUT TOP MANAGEMENT'S ATTITUDE TOWARD THE DP DEPARTMENT

	DP MANAGE-MENT %
Don't Understand What We Do	30
Overanalyze Finances/Tight Financial Control	6
Expectations Too High	4
Failure to Meet Deadlines	4
Believe They Can Do Without Us	4
All Others	4
None/Nothing/No Complaints	38
Don't Know/No Answer	10

TABLE 20

WHAT IS LIKED MOST ABOUT THE DP DEPARTMENT?

	TOTAL %	DP MANAGE- MENT %	TOP MANAGE- MENT %
WORK (NET)	36	24	48
Quick/Fast Response	12	2	22
Efficient	6	—	12
Provide Information/ Data	6	2	10
Current/Up-to-date Technology	5	10	—
Dedication/Loyalty	4	4	4
Organized	3	4	2
The Work (Unspecified)	2	2	2
Reliable	2	—	4
Productive	1	—	2
Accurate	1	—	2
ENVIRONMENT (NET)	28	32	24
Cooperative/Anxious to Please/Willing- ness to Help	14	10	18
Relaxed Environ- ment/Atmosphere	6	12	—
Flexibility	6	6	6

	TOTAL %	DP MANAGE-MENT %	TOP MANAGE-MENT %
Size/Small	2	4	—
All Other Environment Mentions	5	10	—
PEOPLE (NET)	16	22	10
The People	9	12	6
Management	5	6	4
All Other People Mentions	3	4	2
MISCELLANEOUS			
Challenges	13	22	4
Opportunities	3	6	—
All Other Miscellaneous Mentions	11	12	10
Nothing	3	—	6
Don't Know/No Answer	5	4	6

TABLE 21

WHAT IS LIKED LEAST ABOUT THE DP DEPARTMENT?

	TOTAL %	DP MANAGE-MENT %	TOP MANAGE-MENT %
COMMUNICATION (NET)	13	2	24
Inability to Communicate	13	2	24
WORK (NET)	11	6	16
Slow Completing Tasks/ Takes Too Much Time	6	2	10
Backlog/Not Stay on Schedule	3	—	6
No Attention to Quality	2	2	2
All Other Work Mentions	1	2	—
MISCELLANEOUS			
Budget/Finances/ Budget Overruns/ Size of Budget	6	6	6
Unrealistic Expecta-tions/Too Many Things to Do	5	10	—

	TOTAL %	DP MANAGE-MENT %	TOP MANAGE-MENT %
Management Doesn't Understand Us/Lacks Understanding	5	8	2
DP's Inability to See Issue in Top Management	5	—	10
Behind in Technology/ Not Current/Not Up-to-date	5	8	2
Costs/Charges	4	—	8
Don't Know if They're Operating/Running Correctly	3	2	4
Understaffed	3	4	2
Produce a Lot of Unused Data	3	—	6
They Don't See Project from Users' Perspective	2	4	—
Odd Hours	2	4	—
Not Flexible	2	4	—
Too Much Paperwork	1	—	2
DP Produces a Lot of Paper but Not Much of Importance	1	—	2

	TOTAL %	DP MANAGE- MENT %	TOP MANAGE- MENT %
All Other Miscellaneous Mentions	9	10	8
Nothing Disliked	17	20	14
Don't Know/No Answer	9	14	4

TABLE 22

VOCATION RANKING IN TERMS OF IMAGE AMONG CORPORATE LEADERS

	TOTAL %	DP MANAGE- MENT %	TOP MANAGE- MENT %
DATA-PROCESSING MANAGER			
First	2	2	2
Second	11	14	8
Third	24	30	18
Fourth	31	28	34
Fifth	22	18	26
Sixth	7	4	10
Don't Know	3	4	2
ENGINEER			
First	7	4	10
Second	18	18	18
Third	23	24	22
Fourth	12	12	12
Fifth	26	30	22
Sixth	12	10	14
Don't Know	3	4	2

	TOTAL %	DP MANAGE- MENT %	TOP MANAGE- MENT %
MANAGEMENT ACCOUNTANT			
First	7	12	2
Second	12	10	14
Third	9	6	12
Fourth	15	12	18
Fifth	19	20	18
Sixth	35	36	34
Don't Know	3	4	2
PARTNER IN MAJOR CPA FIRM			
First	47	46	48
Second	10	10	10
Third	5	8	2
Fourth	8	6	10
Fifth	10	8	12
Sixth	17	18	16
Don't Know	2	2	2
PRODUCTION MANAGER			
First	8	8	8
Second	21	28	14
Third	18	8	28

	TOTAL %	DP MANAGE- MENT %	TOP MANAGE- MENT %
Fourth	16	20	12
Fifth	16	14	18
Sixth	18	18	18
Don't Know	3	4	2
SALES MANAGER			
First	27	26	28
Second	25	16	34
Third	18	20	16
Fourth	15	18	12
Fifth	4	6	2
Sixth	8	10	6
Don't Know	3	4	2

TABLE 23

PROBLEMS OF DATA PROCESSORS

	TOTAL %	DP MANAGE- MENT %	TOP MANAGE- MENT %
IN GENERAL, DATA PROCESSORS ARE TOO DP-LANGUAGE AND MACHINE ORIENTED			
Agree Strongly	28	22	34
Agree Somewhat	43	44	42
Neither Agree nor Disagree	13	16	10
Disagree Somewhat	13	14	12
Disagree Strongly	1	2	—
Don't Know	2	2	2
IN GENERAL, DATA PROCESSORS LACK IMAGINATION			
Agree Strongly	5	4	6
Agree Somewhat	17	16	18
Neither Agree nor Disagree	14	6	22
Disagree Somewhat	27	20	34
Disagree Strongly	36	52	20
Don't Know	1	2	—

	TOTAL %	DP MANAGE- MENT %	TOP MANAGE- MENT %
IN GENERAL, DATA PROCESSORS TEND TO BE POOR LISTENERS			
Agree Strongly	7	4	10
Agree Somewhat	27	30	24
Neither Agree nor Disagree	24	22	26
Disagree Somewhat	26	26	26
Disagree Strongly	15	16	14
Don't Know	1	2	—
IN GENERAL, DATA PROCESSORS TEND TO BE POOR COMMUNICATORS			
Agree Strongly	14	6	22
Agree Somewhat	46	48	44
Neither Agree nor Disagree	14	16	12
Disagree Somewhat	20	20	20
Disagree Strongly	6	10	2

	TOTAL %	DP MANAGE-MENT %	TOP MANAGE-MENT %
IN GENERAL, DATA PROCESSORS ARE NOT GOOD DECISION-MAKERS			
Agree Strongly	6	2	10
Agree Somewhat	22	14	30
Neither Agree nor Disagree	17	12	22
Disagree Somewhat	31	40	22
Disagree Strongly	24	32	16
IN GENERAL, DATA PROCESSORS ARE RELATIVELY WEAK IN MANAGERIAL SKILLS			
Agree Strongly	12	8	16
Agree Somewhat	43	38	48
Neither Agree nor Disagree	15	14	16
Disagree Somewhat	24	34	14
Disagree Strongly	6	6	6

TABLE 24

ATTRIBUTES OF A SUCCESSFUL DATA PROCESSOR

	TOTAL %	DP MANAGE- MENT %	TOP MANAGE- MENT %
DATA PROCESSORS SHOULD GENERALLY HAVE THE ABILITY TO GET ALONG WELL WITH PEOPLE			
Agree Strongly	69	74	64
Agree Somewhat	24	20	28
Neither Agree nor Disagree	4	2	6
Disagree Somewhat	3	4	2
Disagree Strongly	—	—	—
DATA PROCESSORS SHOULD HAVE GOOD COMMUNICATION SKILLS			
Agree Strongly	89	90	88
Agree Somewhat	10	10	10
Neither Agree nor Disagree	1	—	2
Disagree Somewhat	—	—	—
Disagree Strongly	—	—	—

	TOTAL %	DP MANAGE- MENT %	TOP MANAGE- MENT %
DATA PROCESSORS SHOULD GENERALLY HAVE A HIGH LEVEL OF TECHNICAL SKILL			
Agree Strongly	46	38	54
Agree Somewhat	44	54	34
Neither Agree nor Disagree	2	2	2
Disagree Somewhat	6	6	6
Disagree Strongly	1	—	2
Don't Know	1	—	2
DATA PROCESSORS NEED TO BE HIGHLY INTELLIGENT			
Agree Strongly	34	26	42
Agree Somewhat	45	52	38
Neither Agree nor Disagree	10	10	10
Disagree Somewhat	9	10	8
Disagree Strongly	1	2	—
Don't Know	1	—	2

TABLE 25

ADVICE TO A DATA PROCESSOR JUST STARTING OUT

	DP MANAGE-MENT %
PERSONALITY (NET)	38
Communicate	26
Relate to People	10
All Other Personality Mentions	2
LEARN (NET)	26
Learn as Much as You Can	16
Learn Technical Skills	12
EXPERIENCE (NET)	14
Business Background	14
Practical Experience	2
MISCELLANEOUS	
Do a Good Job	10
Opportunity Is Unlimited	4
Give Job a Chance	4
Look for Company Doing Well	2

	DP MANAGE-MENT %
All Other Miscellaneous Mentions	10
Nothing/No Advice	4
Don't Know/No Answer	6

INDEX